RAILROAD
SIGNALING

BRIAN SOLOMON

Voyageur Press

Quarto is the authority on a wide range of topics.

Quarto educates, entertains and enriches the lives of our readers—enthusiasts and lovers of hands-on living.

www.quartoknows.com

First published in 2010 by Voyageur Press, an imprint of Quarto Publishing Group USA Inc., 400 First Avenue North, Suite 400, Minneapolis, MN 55401 USA. This edition published 2016. Telephone: (612) 344-8100 Fax: (612) 344-8692

quartoknows.com
Visit our blogs at quartoknows.com

Voyageur Press titles are also available at discounts in bulk quantity for industrial or sales-promotional use. For details contact the Special Sales Manager at Quarto Publishing Group USA Inc., 400 First Avenue North, Suite 400, Minneapolis, MN 55401 USA.

ISBN: 978-0-7603-3881-0

The Library of Congress has cataloged the hardcover edition as follows:

Solomon, Brian, 1966–
         Railway signaling / by Brian Solomon.
         p.cm.
         ISBN 0-7603-1360-1 (hc. : alk. Paper)
                 1. Railroads—signaling. I. Title.
         TF615.S695 2003
         625.1'65—dc21
2003056107

Front cover: General Railway Signal searchlights displaying "approach" pierce the evening fog at Brookfield, Wisconsin, on the old Milwaukee Road. The searchlights' focused beams made the signals visible at great distances. *Brian Solomon*

Frontispiece: A General Railway Signal twin-head searchlight signal at the entrance to CTC territory on the old Burlington (now Burlington Northern Santa Fe) at Aurora, Illinois. The sign on the signal informs crews that CTC rules are in effect. It is crucial that operating people know which rules apply, as this may affect how signals are interpreted. *Brian Solomon*

Title pages: Colorlight signals protect the crossing of Conrail's former Boston & Albany mainline with the Central Vermont at Palmer, Massachusetts. This view looks northward on the CV. *Brian Solomon*

Table of contents: Some railroads used a red over lunar white for a "restricting" aspect at the entrance to sidings to indicate that a train should take the siding. A "restricting" would be used on unbonded sidings. Because the signal cannot convey track occupancy, a train must proceed onto the siding at restricted speed, prepared to stop short of trains or obstructions. This photo was made on Wisconsin Central's former Soo Line mainline at Duplainville, Wisconsin, in April 1996. *Brian Solomon*

Back cover, top: At 5:50 P.M. on April 16, 1979, an SP westbound ascends the east slope of Beaumont Hill at the Mons Crossovers. SP favored cantilever signal bridges, which at this location displayed green over dark for the "clear" aspect rather than the more common green over red often displayed at two-head searchlight signals. In 2002, Union Pacific reworked and resignaled this line. *J. D. Schmid*
Back cover, bottom: An operator stands ready to hand up orders to a westbound Nickel Plate Road freight led by a Berkshire type 772 at North East, Pennsylvania. In the United States, timetable and train order rules authorized operations on many lines. *Jim Shaughnessy*

Editor: Dennis Pernu
Designer: Rochelle Schultz

Printed in USA

CONTENTS

INTRODUCTION...6

ACKNOWLEDGMENTS...8

1 EARLY HISTORY...16

2 LATER HISTORY...44

3 MANUAL BLOCK...68

4 TOWERS AND INTERLOCKING...78

5 AUTOMATIC BLOCK...94

6 CENTRALIZED TRAFFIC CONTROL...118

7 TRAIN CONTROL AND CAB SIGNALING...136

8 GRADE CROSSING SIGNALS...144

GLOSSARY...156

BIBLIOGRAPHY...158

INDEX...160

ACKNOWLEDGMENTS

MY INTEREST in railway signaling dates back to my first impressions of railway operations. In 1972, when I was six years old, Bill Garrison, then working for Penn-Central, gave my father and me a personal tour of New York's Grand Central Terminal that included a visit to one of its large control towers. There I experienced firsthand interlocking signals at work. Bill also gave me a copy of a 1937 New York Central rulebook that has been a treasured possession for many years. This well-worn, canvas-covered book has inspired as many questions as it answered.

Since that time, I have studied signal operations on many railways in a score of countries around the world and have visited dozens of signal towers, dispatching offices, and signaling centers. My interests have included the study of traditional mechanical signaling, semaphores, searchlights, position-lights, grade-crossing protection, and more modern technology. The difficulty with writing this book has been in condensing a vast field of knowledge into roughly 45,000 words and 100 photographs.

My own collection of railway signal photos numbers well over 1,000 images, and I have had the pleasure of reviewing outstanding images taken by many other photographers. In researching the text, I have read many books on elements of signaling practice as well as signaling journals, railroad instruction manuals, rulebooks, and employee timetables. This is a detailed, fascinating, and multifaceted subject. I have spoken with many authorities on signaling and found that each has his own special niche of expertise. It has been a challenge to meld information from various perspectives into a coherent and interesting text. I have chosen to focus the text on the developmental history of signals as well as general applications of different types of signaling systems.

In some cases I've invented simple examples, to help the reader comprehend the basic working of signal systems. Simplified basic examples can offer an advantage over real examples, for two reasons. Despite efforts to standardize signal practices and rules, there is a seemingly infinite variety in the application of signal technology. As a result, virtually every signal installation has its own set of peculiarities, making it difficult to give a general example using a specific situation.

Second, inventing an example allows for the selection of names, train symbols, and directions that present a simplified arrangement, which aids comprehension. To balance the generalized examples, I have listed some specific applications while providing photographs of real examples with detailed captions. Since signaling has many specialized terms and special definitions of words, I have compiled a glossary.

Many people helped me in my study of signals, without whom this book could never have been possible. Numerous signal maintainers, operators, dispatchers, signal engineers, train crews, railway officials, and other signaling enthusiasts have provided me with tours and information and have answered my endless list of questions.

My father, Richard Jay Solomon, helped in many ways—he gave me the use of his extensive library, bought rare and unusual signal documents and hardware, and helped with proofreading and tech support. My mother, Maureen, tolerated what she found is a particularly unusual aspect of the railroad field. My brother, Seán, accompanied me on tours of signal towers in West Virginia and Maryland, where we spent many days talking with railroaders about their jobs and adventures.

Special thanks to Pat Yough, who generously lent me documents and literature, helped track down technical information, set up interviews, and provided photos. Thanks to Mike Abalos and Marshall Beecher for signal tours of Chicago and Wisconsin. Thanks also to Markku Pulkkinen for arranging tours of signaling facilities in Finland and Sweden and providing lodging, transportation, and translation.

The staff of Iarnród Éireann (Irish Rail), especially Kevin Walker and Oliver Doyle, have been extremely helpful in many ways, providing me with access, explanations, and literature on the workings of both traditional and modern signal systems in Ireland. The members of the Irish

Railway Record Society allowed me unrestricted use of their library and answered many questions on signal systems around the world. Preserved railways in Britain, including the Keighley & Worth Valley Railway, East Lancashire Railway, Mid-Hants Railway, Bala Lakes Railway, and Great Central Railway, allowed me to visit active restored signal boxes (towers) to observe antique signal practices.

Jon Roma, editor of the *Home Signal* newsletter, provided tours of Chicagoland signaling, answered numerous technical questions, and supplied some caption information. T. S. Hoover provided information on Baltimore & Ohio signal towers and traveled with me on many photographic expeditions. John Hankey provided a greater understanding of the development of the railroad industry in America as well as tours of the B&O and greater Baltimore.

Over the years, Harry Vallas offered much detail on the particulars of New Haven Railroad signaling practices and peculiarities. A fortuitous chance meeting with Alstom's Jeff Power onboard Amtrak's *Lake Shore Limited* resulted in a detailed technical discussion of signal topics. Jeff also assisted with proofreading and technical wording.

Doug Eisele inspired my interest in Union Switch & Signal Style-S semaphores, helped with my understanding of signal mechanisms, and brought me on numerous quests to seek out signals along the former Erie and New York Central routes. Brad Hellman furthered my knowledge of Southern Pacific signal practices and US&S Style-B semaphores. Mark Hemphill helped with research on SP practice and the development of CTC and encouraged an excursion along the old Alton Route to photograph color-position lights.

Harvey Glickenstein, Walter Zullig, Charles R. Tipton, Jr., and Jim Sinclair helped with technical queries. Tim Doherty lent me signal literature and photographs. John Gruber has been extremely helpful in a great many ways, assisting with original research, organizing meetings, and providing transport, lodging, and photographs.

Special thanks to all the photographers who offered and lent material, each of whom is credited with the photograph, among them Steve Smedley, Pete Ruesch, J.D. Schmid and Tom Kline. Jim Shaughnessy, H. Bentley Crouch, Fred Matthews, J. R. Quinn, Bob's Photos, and Jay Williams provided historical images. Mike Gardner provided me the use of his photographic studio and darkroom and lent photographic technical expertise.

I have traveled with numerous fellow photographers who assisted in my photography and lent their expertise in various ways as well as providing transport, directions, and maps. These included Ross Valentine, Brian Plant, Pete Ruesch, Tom Danneman, Mike Danneman, Mel Patrick, Brian Jennison, J. D. Schmid, Mike Gardner, Tim Doherty, Joe McMillan, Tim Hensch, Scott Bontz, Blair Kooistra, Norman Yellin, John Peters, Joe Snopek, John Gruber, Dick Gruber, Brian Rutherford, David Hegarty, Tony Gray, Mark Hodge, Colm O'Callaghan, Howard Ande, Robert A. Buck, Don Marson, G. S. Pitarys, Bill Linley, Chris Burger, Vic Neves, Dave Stanley, Hal Miller, Dean Sauvola, Carl Swanson, Don Gulbrandsen, David Monte Verde, Dave Burton, Gerald Hook, Danny Johnson, and F. L. Becht.

Diarmaid Collins of Dublin, Ireland, and Compleat Communications of Monson, Massachusetts, provided original graphics. Special thanks to the staff at the Monson, Massachusetts, Post Office for locating lost slides.

Thanks to Dennis Pernu and everyone at MBI Publishing for their help in editing, design, layout, production, and marketing.

Hundreds of sources have been consulted, and every effort has been made to provide correct and accurate information and the highest-quality photographs. Ideally a book would be entirely free from inaccuracies, and it is my hope that this book is as accurate and up to date as possible. In some situations, conflicting data and reports have put absolute accuracy in question. In these cases, I have tried to qualify data accordingly. Errors, should they appear, are entirely my own and not those of the many specialists who have assisted me. It is my hope that all who read this book enjoy it and learn something about the diverse and fascinating world of railway signals.

—*Brian Solomon*
March 2003

INTRODUCTION

THE RAILWAY originated in Britain, evolving from an industrial tramway used by quarries and collieries to a general-purpose transport system. Most of the principal elements that made the railway possible, including tracks, locomotives, and basic practices of operation, were established in Britain. Logically, this study of American railway signaling begins in Britain, where many of the basic practices originated. Understanding the fundamentals of nineteenth-century British signaling practice helps put American developments in context, as well as those of numerous other countries. During the height of the railway-building era, the British colonial empire extended around the globe. As a result, British railway practices were established in many places. Many railways reflect the direct influence of nineteenth-century British signaling practices today, and in some places vintage signal equipment remains in service.

Although British and American railways evolved differently, they have influenced each other in many ways, and certainly early American railway practice was more affected by developments in Britain than in any other country. Detailed study of modern British signaling practice is a topic in its own right, one that has been covered extensively by other publications.

Looking toward the west switch at Solitude, Utah, along the old Denver & Rio Grande Western, a General Railway Signal color light displays "clear." D&RGW adopted this type of color light in the 1920s. Brian Solomon

RAILWAY EVOLUTION

THE FIRST practical steam locomotives were developed in the early nineteenth century for industrial tramways. The railway took a step forward in 1821, when British Parliament authorized the construction of the Stockton & Darlington, a line built by George Stephenson that would become the first steam-powered public railway. It opened in 1825. Stephenson went on to engineer an even more significant railway project, the Liverpool & Manchester, which opened in 1829.

British developments quickly attracted the attention of American companies, who dispatched teams of engineers to study railway practice. Beginning in the late 1820s, several American railway companies were formed. They imported British railway technology—in many cases quite literally, shipping locomotives and rails across the Atlantic. The standard American track gauge—4 feet, 8.5 inches—is the same one used by Stephenson. This gauge has become the standard used by most railways in Britain, America, and many countries in Western Europe.

The back of a General Railway Signal semaphore blade on the Montana Rail Link's former Northern Pacific at Toston, Montana. On many lines, the backs of semaphore blades were painted black with white chevrons, to distinguish them from the front. Tom Kline

However, different conditions in American topography, business practice, and transport requirements altered railway development in the United States in the formative period. Where British railways tended to be well financed and highly engineered, American railways often struggled for funds in their early years and tended to be more lightly engineered.

American railways also faced more formidable geographical obstacles, having to cross large rivers, mountains, and vast stretches of unpopulated land. British railways were built with gentle gradients and avoided grade-level crossing with highways and other railway lines. Also their rights-of-way were normally fenced off. By contrast,

🎧 Union Switch & Signal Style-B lower-quadrant semaphores show the track is clear along Southern Pacific's Tucumcari Line at Polly, New Mexico, on January 17, 1994. Brian Solomon

American lines often faced prolonged and sometimes steep gradients, frequent level highway crossings and railway crossings, and generally did not fence their rights-of-way.

The relatively compact geography of Britain, combined with dense population and numerous well-established cities and industrial areas, plus existing transport networks in the form of canals and well-maintained roads, gave many British railways a healthy traffic base from the beginning. While some American lines on the East Coast enjoyed similar settings, many lines especially those built across the Midwest, Plains, and Far West suffered from light traffic. These lines pioneered the way west and brought settlement with them. Distances were great, populations small, but the potential for growth seemed unlimited.

The attitudes of American people differed from those of the British, too. Interpretation of law was more relaxed. The emphasis was on individual responsibility and a belief in making one's own destiny (or doom, as the case may be.)

These differences, combined with different attitudes toward technology, all contributed toward the diverging paths of railway development, and thus railway signal development, in Britain and America. Although British and American signaling have evolved to achieve similar goals, they do so using different philosophies. Neither practice grew up in a vacuum, and there was considerable technological cross-fertilization across the Atlantic.

British signaling was more highly developed at an early stage, but legislation encouraging, then mandating, the implementation of signaling in Britain effectively stalled development. American signaling, by contrast, was relatively primitive through most of the 1800s but at the end of that century began to advance rapidly and took good

Two-arm, three-aspect Union Switch & Signal Style-B lower-quadrant semaphores display "clear." This style of signal was standard on the Southern Pacific until the 1930s, when the company began using US&S searchlights for new installations. The Style-B lower-quadrant semaphore remained a symbol of safety on SP until the 1980s. *Brian Solomon*

On this signal, the blade on the left shows "clear," meaning that a train traveling in that direction has no orders. The blade on the right indicates that a train traveling in the other direction must stop for orders. A train must heed only the red and white blade, as the black and white one is used for traffic in the opposite direction. *Brian Solomon*

advantage of technological innovations. Years after British signaling practices and hardware had become relatively standardized, American signaling continued to become more complex, as various railroads continued to implement their own standards.

Operating practices differed, with American railroad operations tended toward running fewer but longer, heavier trains. British railways suffered from a restrictive loading gauge established in the early years of railway building, and the numerous tunnels and over-bridges often made improvements to the British loading gauge prohibitively expensive.

Widespread use of signaling at an earlier time had the effect of fixing passing sidings (known as passing loops in Britain) at relatively short lengths, which has limited train lengths in Britain to this day. The constraints of train size and length had profound implications for locomotive and train development. Locomotives were relatively compact unlike late-era American steam, which was characterized by enormous machines.

Some American railways moved toward speed signaling, rather than route signaling, and the majority of eastern lines had embraced speed signaling by the end of the steam era. Where route signaling simply indicates a diverging route, speed signaling is used to govern the speed of trains through interlockings and sometimes at restrictive signals. Governing speed with signals has both advantages and disadvantages. While speed signaling involves greater complexity and more aspects, it provides locomotive engineers with added warning and allows for operational flexibility when trains of widely varying speed and weight operate over the same lines. Today, on some American railroads, slow-moving 14,000-ton coal trains and high-speed passenger trains may need to use the same sets of tracks. Speed signaling can provide necessary and detailed information to safely minimize the delay of trains using diverging routes.

American signaling has tended to allow greater flexibility of operations while providing a different level of collision protection than British railways. American railways were quick to adopt a uniform failsafe braking system, in the form of the Westinghouse Airbrake, and all steel equipment, but hesitated to adopt block signaling because of its high cost of operation.

American signaling has followed common trends in American railroad practice and has been driven by the desire to use technology to replace people. Many modern signaling advances have been aimed at reducing employment by increasing the work a single operator can do safely, thus maintaining safety while lowering costs. New systems are not necessarily safer but are often cheaper to operate. American signal control has followed a path toward ever greater centralization and component miniaturization.

Railway signals are essentially communication devices, and railway signaling is essentially a simple but precise language. As with spoken language, the signal system has words, but only a few words, and they have clearly defined meanings. With signaling, the signal hardware is used to convey aspects, and the aspects are given to convey specific instructions. Comparing signals to spoken language, the hardware is the tool for transmitting the words, the aspects are the words, and indications conveyed by aspects are the definitions of the words. To add clarity, aspects are put in quotes, so we say a signal displays an "approach" aspect. This is necessary to avoid confusion with hardware. An approach signal is a distant signal to a home signal and can display an "approach" aspect.

What can make the study of different signaling systems confusing is that each railway may assign different definitions to signal aspects. This is similar to how different languages assign different definitions to the same words. In signaling, even the most basic red light can have different meanings on different railroads, depending on how each company interprets it. One line may call red a "stop" aspect, another "stop and proceed."

Another confusing element is the great variety of signal hardware used to display aspects. In the United States alone, more than a half-dozen different styles of signal hardware are in use, as well as several styles of obsolete hardware. Although various hardware may convey different aspects, the indications of these aspects may be the same. An upper-quadrant semaphore displays "clear" with a vertically raised arm, a lower-quadrant semaphore with an arm lowered at a diagonal, and a modern color-light signal with a green light. With all three types of hardware, "clear" has precisely the same indication, meaning "proceed." Some aspects, such as two yellow lights (one over the other), can have different meanings on different railroads, depending on the railroad's rules.

Although comparing different systems may cause confusion, in actual practice railroad operating people working on a specific line shouldn't be confused. Railroaders must have a clear understanding of the signal aspects

It's February 15, 2003, at Flint, Indiana, where Norfolk Southern signal maintainer Jim Sinclair is carefully cleaning snow off westbound signal lenses. The temperature is in the low twenties Fahrenheit, and the wind is blowing at a steady 30 mph; this is not a job for the faint of heart. Pete Ruesch

(and the information those aspects convey) for their line. They have learned from their company rulebook and follow their rules accordingly. How this information is interpreted on other lines is not relevant to them and thus need not present confusion. Also, while a railroad may list a great variety of aspects in its rulebook, in their daily work, railroaders will encounter only a portion of these aspects and will become familiar with them, so they will rarely be in doubt as to the interpretation of signals.

The word "signaling" has two spellings. It is listed as one of more than thirty spelling differences between American usage and British usage. So in British publications, the

A semaphore conveys aspects by the position of its arm. This Union Switch & Signal Style-T semaphore on the Santa Fe at Model, Colorado, displays "clear." One difficulty with semaphores was displaying aspects at night. Most railroads overcame this by adding colored lights to augment the position of the blade. Brian Solomon

"signalling" spelling is always used. It is also used in this book when British documents are quoted.

Signal systems balance three basic premises in their design and operation: safety, cost, and capacity. All signaling systems are a compromise. Although the cry of "safety first" is often heard in regard to signaling, it should be remembered that this was originally aimed at the railroad employee as an admonishment to adhere to company rules. John A. Droege points out in his 1916 book *Passenger Terminals and Trains* that the time-honored safety principle was "in case of doubt, take the safe course and run no risks." In regard to signal installation, an appropriate slogan may

be "Safety within the parameters of normal operation and at practical cost."

Signals have been installed to ensure safety but are often also used to increase line capacity without incurring unnecessary risk of collision. The high cost of implementing sophisticated automatic train control or positive train control systems has made these systems prohibitive for use on most lines. Signal systems are designed to provide a reasonable margin of safety at affordable cost. A railway doesn't want to spend anymore than it has to for safe operations, yet as history has demonstrated, neither can it afford to spend less than demanded for safe operations.

The earliest railways had little need for complex signaling, because there were relatively few trains, and these were lightweight and traveled at slow speeds. As a result, possibilities for collisions were few, and the potential for damage was relatively low.

AS THE FREQUENCY, weight, and speed of trains increased, the potential for dangerous collisions became a problem. Early railways ran trains using a strict schedule and clear rules for operation. Timetable and rulebook operation worked well most of the time. It must be understood that in the 1820s and 1830s, before the telegraph or telephone was invented, there was no simple method for communicating the location of trains. Once a train left the station, it was out of reach. The only way to run a railway was strictly by the rules. Double-track had the advantage of increasing capacity while minimizing the potential for head-on collisions.

The Liverpool and Manchester was perhaps the first company to use a signal system. According to Richard Blythe, author of *Danger Ahead,* the Liverpool and Manchester positioned railway policemen along its line. Among their duties were to keep people off the tracks and indicate to passing trains the condition of the line ahead, using arm signals. An outstretched arm indicated the line was clear, while arms at the side indicated a problem. In addition, they raised a red flag when a train had paused for a station stop.

Blythe indicates that elements of Liverpool and Manchester's signaling were derived from marine practice, including displaying a revolving lamp at the back of a

Lightly used crossings were sometimes protected by simple "tiltboard" signals. Sparta Junction, New Jersey, photographed in October 1963, was the crossing of the Lehigh and Hudson River and the New York, Susquehanna & Western.
Richard Jay Solomon

train at night. The lamp featured red and blue lenses. By 1834, the Liverpool and Manchester is believed to have initiated the use of fixed signals, consisting of a post with an iron bar that could be rotated to display a red flag. If the flag was perpendicular to the rail, it indicated "danger," but if it was parallel to the track, the line was assumed to be "clear." Other early railways adopted similar fixed signals that used rotating paddles and boards.

The first use of fixed signals in the United States is credited to the Newcastle and Frenchtown Railroad, a 17-mile line that connected its namesake cities in Delaware and Maryland, respectively. According to Brignano and McCullough in *The Search for Safety* (a book on signals put out by American signal manufacturer Union Switch & Signal), the line erected a network of masts at stations along the line about three miles apart.

Initially, black and white flags were hoisted up the masts, but these proved ineffective, and the railway subsequently used balls (sometimes described as baskets that resembled balls). If a white ball was raised, the train was on time. A black ball raised meant that the train had left late. When the train had departed, the ball was lowered halfway down the mast. Unlike modern signals, these balls simply indicated a train's progress and do not appear to have actually governed the movement of trains on the line. As with all early signals, they were operated manually.

In Britain, Isambard K. Brunel's famous Great Western Railway, known for its 7-foot gauge tracks (technically, 7 feet, 1/4 inch between the rails), was another early user of the ball signal. In his book *Red for Danger,* L. T. C. Rolt explains that a ball signal was used at Reading to indicate

One of the earliest railroad signals was a ball on a line. This type of signal was later used at stations and grade-level railroad crossings. The last such signal to be in regular service is at Whitefield, New Hampshire, where the former Boston & Maine crossed the Maine Central Mountain Division.
Brian Solomon

Ball signals were used at stations to give trains permission to depart, and also at grade-level crossings with other railway lines, sometimes described as "diamond crossings," to indicate which train had the right to cross. With the simplest indications, a raised ball indicated proceed, and a lowered ball indicated stop. At locations featuring complex junctions, ball signals could be used to display more complex indications by hoisting multiple balls.

Boston & Maine Railroad Time Table No. 41, effective June 21, 1946, describes the indications of its ball signals: "Each engineman approaching the crossing will bring his engine to a stop at some point within one thousand (1,000) feet from the crossing. If the signal is right, he may then proceed."

At White River Junction, Vermont, which had a complicated four-way junction involving a diamond crossing with Central Vermont Railway, the rules were more complicated:

> One ball or one red light will allow trains from Central Vermont Ry. (Northern Division) or movements from the west to cross.
>
> Two balls or two red lights will allow trains from the Concord-White River Jct. Main Line (N.H. Division) or movements from the east to cross, but switching may be done over crossing, east and west on two balls or two red lights.
>
> Three balls or three red lights will allow trains from the Berlin-White River Jct. Line (N.H. Division), or movements from north to cross, but switching may be done over crossing north or south on three balls or three red lights.
>
> Four balls or four red lights will allow trains from Central Vermont Ry. (Southern Division) or movements from the south to cross.
>
> When no signal is displayed all trains or movements approaching the diamond must stop. Any movement over diamond when no signal is displayed will be made only on the authority of the signalman.

Although other types of signaling hardware superseded the ball signal, the ball's legacy lives on. Ball signals such as those described above were common at level railway crossings in northern New England until the end of the steam era. Most were replaced by the mid-1960s, but the lone

when the station was clear. Rolt reproduces the railway's March 1840 regulation which reads, "A Signal Ball will be seen at the entrance to Reading station when the Line is right for the train to go in. If the Ball is not visible the Train must not pass it."

In America, ball signals were typically equipped with lanterns for night indications. In later years, the balls were made from sectional copper rings and were typically painted either red or black. The ball (and lanterns) would be hoisted into position using a rope-and-pulley mechanism similar to that employed on a common clothesline but arranged vertically, parallel to the supporting mast.

signal at Whitefield, New Hampshire, has survived into modern times. The use of ball signals gave way to the term "highball," which meant proceed, and in casual speech, railroaders will still use "highball" when it's time to leave the station. Another derivation of the word was used to describe a locomotive engineer who ran fast.

Boston & Maine used a multiple-ball signal at its diamond crossing at White River Junction, Vermont. The number of balls (or lights) displayed authorized movements across the diamond in different directions. "Four balls," as displayed here, authorizes a movement from the Central Vermont Railway or from the south to cross. On July 27, 1957, Boston & Maine GP7 1559 is heading northward toward Woodsville and Berlin, New Hampshire. Jim Shaughnessy

BIRTH OF
THE SEMAPHORE

Ships had long used systems of visual semaphore signals to communicate information. In 1841, Charles Hutton Gregory adapted a fixed semaphore for use on the London and Croydon Railway. This is often considered the first use of a fixed semaphore on a railway line and is an antecedent to most modern signaling. By the late 1840s, several prominent British railways had adopted semaphores for use on their lines. These were three-position lower-quadrant semaphores.

A semaphore is described by the number of positions its blade displays and the positions the blade occupies. With a lower-quadrant semaphore, the blade is lowered from the horizontal, which is considered the most restrictive position. A three-position semaphore's most favorable position is the vertical. A midway position, usually at about the 45-degree mark, gives an intermediate cautionary aspect.

Upper-quadrant semaphores were developed much later and feature the blade raised from a horizontal position

In June 1960, a New Haven Railroad EP-4 electric leads a New York–bound passenger train. The New Haven used left-handed upper-quadrant semaphores, contrary to standard practice. These short-arm semaphores were installed at Bridgeport, Connecticut, in 1912 to replace Hall disc signals. In electrified territory, New Haven's semaphores were powered by alternating current and used high-intensity electric lamps designed to be dimmed at night. Richard Jay Solomon

On January 24, 1981, Chicago & North Western train No. 391, led by a pair of Electro-Motive SD45s, crossed Milwaukee Road's Moline-to-Savanna, Illinois, line at East Clinton. At that time, this crossing was still protected by electrically operated semaphores. Many lines used a squared-off blade colored red with a white stripe to indicate a home signal. Such a signal indicated an absolute "stop" when displayed in the horizontal position, as shown here. John Leopard

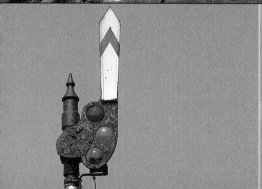

"CLEAR"

"APPROACH"

"STOP AND PROCEED"

These views of a Union Switch & Signal Style-S upper-quadrant semaphore on the former Erie Railroad at Tioga, New York, show the signal's three aspects, from least restrictive to most restrictive: "clear," "approach," and "stop and proceed." The Erie followed the American Association of Railroads' standard recommended practice, using pointed-end yellow blades with a black chevron for intermediate automatic block semaphores. This signal was fitted with a number plate, needed to qualify a permissive signal. Brian Solomon

to indicate less restrictive aspects. On typical early three-position lower-quadrant semaphores used in Britain, the blade actually lowered into a slot in the mast to indicate "proceed."

Until the early years of the twentieth century, the colors used to display fundamental signal aspects at night were different from what they are today. In Britain, typical signals used red for "stop"—a color that has retained its indication—but a green light indicated "caution," while a white light was used for the "clear" indication. So a "clear" aspect indicated proceed. It is not known whether the term "a clear signal" originated because of its use of a white light or because it implied that the track ahead was unoccupied. Perhaps the dual meaning of the word was just a convenient coincidence. In any case, the use of a white light for "clear" made good sense in the early days.

Since red, green, and white were the most common colors used for night signals in Britain, the practice there inspired similar practice in the United States. However,

prior to the establishment of signaling standards, every railway had its own rules, with numerous variations between different carriers' interpretations of specific aspects and their corresponding indications.

In Britain, semaphores were erected on tall masts, so the blade could be clearly seen against the sky. A fixed semaphore had advantages: a locomotive engineer knew exactly where to look for the signal, and it could be made much taller than a man, so it could be seen more clearly from a greater distance.

In the early years the masts were made of wood, but later, iron masts were favored. Initially, signalmen manually operated the signals from the base. Since the natural weight of the signal would cause it drop into the clear position, counterweights were introduced for failsafe operation. Counterweights would force the blade into the horizontal position in case of a human failure or technical problem. Later semaphores were adapted for remote mechanical operation and, much later, for electric operation.

A train order signal did not provide track authority but indicated when a train should stop to collect train orders. Railroads used many styles of train order signals, which were typically located at passenger stations or towers. This one was photographed after a winter storm at Morris, Illinois, along the Rock Island. Steve Smedley

In the latter half of the nineteenth century, no instrument of technology was considered so utilitarian as to be undeserving of proper decor. The style of semaphores evolved to incorporate Victorian-era ornamentation. Styles of the blades and masts were refined. The masts were topped with ornate finials, giving the signals a touch of class while offering protection from birds that might be inclined to rest on top of them and foul the blades.

In early British practice, semaphores provided warnings by time interval systems. A signalman would display his signal in the clear position until a train passed, then railway rules instructed him to keep it in the stop position for a specific length of time. If another train came along, it was required to wait until the interval had passed. In some situations, after a length of time, the signalman could lower the semaphore to display a "caution," to allow a train to proceed at reduced speed. Railway rules varied on whether signals should be normally kept in the "stop" position or the "clear" position.

The use of three-position lower-quadrant-style semaphores with slotted masts was once common in British railway block signal practice but fell out of favor in Britain following a disastrous wreck at Abbots Ripton on the Great Northern Railway in 1876. A snowstorm clogged the slots, trapping the semaphore blades in the clear position, preventing signalmen from displaying warning signals to an express passenger train. A coal train was stopped on the line ahead, and the express collided with it at speed. Making matters worse, the signals were still stuck in the clear position, and, despite alternative measures to warn trains of the wreck, there was a second collision.

According to Richard Blythe in *Danger Ahead*, the two crashes killed 13 people and injured many more, including several prominent people. The Russian ambassador as well as some Great Northern directors had been riding on the wrecked trains. Subsequent investigations revealed the flaws of using slotted masts. After that, two-position lower-quadrant semaphores became standard in Britain. These signals displayed a horizontal aspect for "stop" and a lowered angled aspect for "clear." Another consequence of the Abbots Ripton wreck was the adoption in British practice of normally displaying signals at "stop" until necessary to show the line clear for a train.

In the United States, three-position lower-quadrant semaphores were commonly used as train order signals but not as block signals. (The principles behind train order operation are described later in the text.) Since train order semaphores did not indicate track conditions and were not used to authorize track occupancy, these signals were normally left in the "clear" position. Restrictive aspects were used to indicate whether a train needed to collect orders (which could authorize track occupancy, among other instructions).

INTERLOCKING SIGNALS

Signals governing the movement of trains fall into several distinct categories, including interlocking signals, block signals, and special warning signals. Interlocking signals are those under human control and are used to govern movements at junctions, crossings, and crossovers—places where tracks intersect and trains need to move over diverging routes.

The first application of lever controlled signals is often credited to an installation designed by Charles Hutton Gregory, at Bricklayers Arms Junction on the London and Croydon Railway in 1843–44. (As previously mentioned, Gregory had also introduced the semaphore.) This represented a consolidation of signal and switch control to a central point at the junction. Centralization is a fundamental component of interlocking installations, and over the last 160 years, railway interlockings have followed a pattern of ever greater consolidation of control.

A gear-operated train order signal at the preserved station in Golden, Colorado, on the grounds of the Colorado Railroad Museum. An operator would set this signal from inside the station to indicate that a train needed to stop for train orders. Tom Kline

Another crucial element of interlocking signals is the predetermined sequence of actions designed to prevent the arrangement of conflicting routes. John Saxby, a foreman with the London, Brighton & South Coast Railway, is credited with the first installation that applied both the mechanized operation of signals and interlocking safeguards. In 1856, following a misrouting incident at Bricklayers Arms Junction, Saxby developed a mechanical lever frame that interlocked the movements of eight signal and six switch levers. He patented his invention and, in 1863, went into business with John Farmer in the manufacture of signal interlocking equipment. Details from Saxby's

1856 patent were reprinted in Brignano & McCullough's *The Search for Safety*:

> I, John Saxby, of Brighton, Sussex, do hereby declare the nature of the said Invention for 'A Mode of Working simultaneously the Points and Signals of Railways at Junctions, to Prevent Accidents,' to be as follows:—
>
> This invention consists of an arrangement of mechanism by which the 'switches' or 'points,' the signal lamps, and the arms of semaphore signals, as used on railways, may be simultaneously actuated by one movement, and in such a manner that the points cannot be wrong when the signals are right, nor the signals wrong when the points are right. Hitherto the signal lamps and arms of the semaphore signal or telegraph have been actuated by one movement of the hand of the signal man, while by an arrangement of stirrups for the feet he was enabled to adjust the 'points;' but this arrangement has led to serious accidents from want of proper connexion between the points which shift the carriage from one line to another, and the signals which indicate to a coming train the safety of proceeding; for while the signals have been right, the points or switches have been wrong, or vice versâ, causing collisions and other accidents. By the simultaneous action of my arrangement much greater certainty and safety are attained, and the use of pedals or stirrups for the feet of the signal man dispensed with.

While a vast improvement over non-interlocked junctions, Saxby's early interlocking device (known as a lever frame) exhibited a number of basic flaws. One was no mechanism ensured that switch points followed a full movement. It was possible to move the points into a dangerous halfway position while still being able to clear the appropriate signal. In *Danger Ahead*, Richard Blythe explains that in 1859, Austin Chambers devised an improved interlocking that overcame this problem. This was installed at Kentish Town Junction on the North London Railway.

Over the next decade, Saxby and others made important improvements to mechanical interlocking frames. Blythe notes that in 1870, the development of the tappet interlocking was patented by J. J., J. J. F., and W. A. Stevens. This innovation made the construction of complex interlocking frames possible. In 1874, Saxby introduced an improved lever system known as a "rocker and gridiron," which included a locking latch on the handle. This system

A crossover is a pair of switches that allows a train to cross from one main track to another. This view of "NI" interlocking on the Chicago & North Western shows three sets of crossovers. Note that the middle crossover has the points set to connect the center track with the right-hand track. These are power switches controlled remotely; the switch machines can be seen near each set of points. Brian Solomon

improved the motion of the lever while locking it in place when motion was completed.

These developments paved the way for the interlocking tower, or "signal box," as it is known in Britain. The earliest signal installations were uncovered, and signalmen were sometimes subject to harsh weather in the course of their duties. It was only with the coming of mechanical interlocking frames that signal installations were enclosed, to protect the equipment. Signal installation control was often elevated, to give signalmen a better view of the signals and switches they operated—thus the need for a tower. Not all

A Dublin-bound empty passenger train passes the signal cabin at Athenry, Co. Galway, Ireland, on May 12, 2002. This signal cabin controls the junction of several routes, using traditional mechanical levers to move semaphores and switches. The electric staff system is used to provide track authority. This traditional system is now being replaced with Centralized Traffic Control. Brian Solomon

signal towers were actual towers, however. Remote locations were often operated from cabins on the ground or from a bay in a passenger or freight station.

The first known application of interlocking signals in America was an 1870 installation at Trenton, New Jersey, on a Pennsylvania Railroad component, United New Jersey Canal and Railroad Companies. This work is credited to Ashbel Welch, the line's president and chief engineer, who also introduced the first block working in the United States (discussed later). Like an earlier generation of railway engineers, Welch had traveled to England to observe developments there. He was especially impressed by the development of the interlocking tower and imported the basic concepts of interlocking for use on his lines.

According to the PRR centennial edition of *The Mutual Magazine*, the second interlocking in America was

Detail of a General Railway Signal relay box. Brian Soloman

25

installed on the Pennsylvania Railroad at Newark Junction, New Jersey, in 1875. By 1900, mechanical interlocking towers were a standard feature at railway junctions and crossovers all over the United States. Many railroads imported Saxby & Farmer machines for work in the U.S.A., some of which were still in service into the 1990s. Electropneumatic and all-electric interlocking systems were perfected by 1900, and all-relay installations were introduced in the 1920s. Yet mechanical interlockings were built new through the 1920s, and today, examples of mechanical interlockings are still in service in the United States and around the world. Details of interlocking working is covered in Chapter 4.

TELEGRAPHS

The invention of the electric telegraph was perhaps the most important development in the history of train control. Without electric communication, it was impractical to send information about train operation ahead of a train, making railway operation dependant on timetables and rules. In the early days, when trains ran late, operations sometimes became haphazard and even reckless. There are numerous instances of trains running toward one another on single-track, without any knowledge of where the other was. The relatively slow speeds of the times prevented most serious accidents; when accidents did happen, they tended to be relatively minor.

The first telegraphs were developed in Britain. Electric telegraphic experiments date back to the second decade of the nineteenth century. At that time, the telegraph was viewed primarily as a military tool. Early experiments were largely unsuccessful in developing a practical telegraph system.

In May 1837, Charles Wheatstone went into business with William Fothergill Cooke to develop telegraphic communications. They received their first British patent in June 1837. Railway applications were then seen as a primary market. Their telegraphic devices used four or five pivoting needles, which swiveled left or right depending on the direction of the current applied to them. The needles would point to different voltage levels and, through an encoding system (similar to the later punched tape telegraphs—which, incidentally, led to modern alphanumeric computer coding), would represent symbols, depending on the needles'

sequence. Multiple needles sped up the transmission by working in parallel.

According to Richard Blythe in *Danger Ahead*, the Cooke and Wheatstone telegraph was used as early as 1837 between Euston and the Camden engine-house to coordinate a portage system of moving trains by ropes up the grade out of London's Euston Station. Cooke was the more gregarious partner. According to Michael A. Vanns in *Signalling in the Age of Steam*, Cooke approached Isambard K. Brunel in 1838 with the idea of setting up telegraph stations on Brunel's Great Western Railway. For about a decade, beginning in mid-1839, Cooke and Wheatstone's, six-wire, five-needle telegraph connected GWR's London Paddington Station with stations at Hanwell and West Drayton. In 1843, a line was extended to Slough. The telegraph was used experimentally to monitor trains traveling over the line but not for the direction of train movements.

Vanns goes on to explain that the first use of a telegraph in governing train movements was on the London & Blackwell Railway in 1840. This short, cable-hauled railway used single-needle telegraph instruments to provide operating information, requiring much less wiring. The success of this operation encourage Cooke, who published a promotional book in 1842 titled *Telegraphic Railways* that illustrated the possibilities of railway operation using telegraphically controlled block sections.

Cooke and Wheatstone improved their telegraph in the mid-1840s with the introduction of a simplified single-wire system that used a natural ground for circuit return. Also in the mid-1840s, a number of British railways had adopted telegraphs for the control of short track sections, typically through single-track tunnels, where a serious crash could have dire ramifications. The Clayton Tunnel on the Brighton Railway was the first such operation, adopting telegraph working in 1841.

During the 1840s, the telegraph caught on quickly for general applications and, at the end of the decade, was

⤸ Mechanical interlocking centralized the control of switches and signals while improving safety by insuring that events occurred in a predetermined order. A mechanical plant, such as Waterford Central on Iarnród Éireann (Irish Rail), uses large mechanical levers to set signals and switches. This job takes both skill and strength. *Brian Solomon*

being used to communicate public messages. Many telegraph companies were established in both Britain and the United States. Railway telegraph operation in Britain allowed for the development of a manual block system, typically using needle instruments that could be used to show the condition of the line while providing a system of communication using bell codes (see Chapter 3).

In America, Samuel Finley Breese Morse, working with Alfred Vail, had developed a telegraph system that worked using electric pulses operating a "sounder" instead of needles. A telegraph key was used to transmit the pulses over the wire. This system used just one wire, with a natural ground for return currents. It was a simpler, cheaper system than the Cooke and Wheatstone telegraph, and for that reason perhaps better suited to American applications.

Morse is probably best known today for the communicating code developed to send telegraphic messages, though evidence indicates that Vail developed the code. By rapidly transmitting sequences of dots and dashes with telegraph keys, telegraph operators could communicate messages over the wire and decode them by merely listening, faster than reading the deflections of a bank of needles.

In the 1840s, Morse convinced the Baltimore & Ohio to allow him to string telegraph wires along the railroad. On May 24, 1844, Morse transmitted a telegraphic message from Washington, D.C., 30 miles to Baltimore, which read, prophetically, "What hath God wrought." This public debut demonstrated the potential of telegraphic communication in the United States.

Several more years passed before the telegraph was used in American railway operation. Instantaneous communication was such a revolutionary concept that it took a while for its full potential to be realized and exploited by the railroads—and, in fact many railroad officials were suspicious and distrustful of telegraph technology in its early days. To some, the telegraph seemed to threaten the railroad. Others saw no need to alter railroad rules. Timetable operation had provided railroad men with a logical and workable system

for the movement of trains that had sufficed for daily operations of the period—if somewhat unreliable, as evidenced by the numerous collisions.

One of the first American railroads to adopt the telegraph was the Erie Railroad, under the direction of superintendent, Charles Minot. According to Robert Luther Thompson in *Wiring a Continent*, Minot developed an interest in the telegraph in 1849 and convinced the railroad's directors to invest in the construction of a telegraph line parallel to the railroad. At the end of 1850, the Erie had a telegraph line from its original eastern terminus at Piedmont, New York, to Goshen.

Minot is often credited with the first application of the telegraph to advance a train contrary to its printed schedule. As legend has it, in June 1851, Minot was riding a westbound passenger express that was scheduled to meet an eastbound at Turners, New York. When the eastbound failed to arrive on schedule, Minot asked the telegrapher in the office at Turners to wire ahead, to see if the eastbound had departed the station at Goshen. On learning that the

By 1860, many American railroads were using the telegraph to issue "train orders" to augment timetable operation. Most stations had a telegraph office, such as this one preserved at Golden, Colorado. Here an operator could communicate with a train dispatcher and other operators. In later years, the telephone supplemented and later replaced the telegraph as a primary means of communication. Brian Solomon

The Boston & Maine operator at East Northfield, Massachusetts, hands up orders to the southbound Central Vermont Railway local running from Brattleboro, Vermont, and Palmer, Massachusetts, on March 12, 1954. The operator has two sets of written orders: one for the head-end crew on the locomotive; the other (seen in his left hand) for the rear-end crew riding in the caboose. Train orders were use to authorize train movements, supplementing or altering operating schedules. Jim Shaughnessy

This view of the Delaware & Hudson station at Watervliet, New York, in June 1913 depicts a common arrangement found in the northeastern United States in that period. Manually operated grade-crossing gates are located at both ends of the station. A train order signal sits on the middle of the station platform, and an interlocking tower can be seen on the right side of the photo. Notice the multiple-arm telegraph poles. These carried many wires needed for communication at the time. Jim Shaughnessy collection

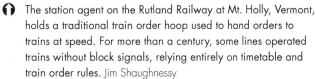

The station agent on the Rutland Railway at Mt. Holly, Vermont, holds a traditional train order hoop used to hand orders to trains at speed. For more than a century, some lines operated trains without block signals, relying entirely on timetable and train order rules. Jim Shaughnessy

The station at Altamont, New York, on the Delaware & Hudson featured a three-position lower-quadrant train order semaphore. The signal is set for a train to stop for orders in one direction but is clear in the other. Beyond are lower-quadrant block semaphores. Notice the dummy mast on the gantry, indicating that these signals do not govern the track on the right. On the left, near the grade crossing, is a watchman's shanty, from which the gates are controlled. A professional photographer made this photo on November 6, 1913. Jim Shaughnessy collection

eastbound had not yet arrived at Goshen, Minot asked the telegrapher to send the following message:

> **To Agent and Operator at Goshen**
> **Hold the train for further orders.**
> **Chas. Minot, Superintendent.**

He then ordered the locomotive engineer of the westbound to proceed to Goshen. According to the story, the engineer, appalled by this violation of timetable rules, refused to take the train on, and Minot ran the train himself.

This story has been passed down over generations and has become one of the standard myths of American railroading. Whether it was actually the first application of the telegraph for railroad operations is unclear. However, the pattern of operation established by Minot became the basis for train order operation—a standard feature of American railroading for more than a hundred years.

By the advent of the Civil War, telegraphic operation had become a common feature on many American railroads. Operations by timetable and train order were the basic methods of safe train operation for most American railways. Train orders could be used to supersede or supplement timetable authority, allowing railroad officials, who became known as dispatchers, to more efficiently regulate the movement of trains over the line. Train order stations were set up at regular intervals, typically at established stations and passing sidings. Telegraph operators would copy orders sent over the wire from the dispatcher on paper and deliver them to trains.

Over the years, the system of timetable and train orders was perfected and refined. Many railroads issued two varieties of orders: those that needed to be signed for by the train crew and those that did not. Orders that required a signature usually restricted authority, so a signature was mandatory to ensure that operating men had received orders and presumably understood those orders.

Orders that did not require a signature could be passed to trains "on the fly,"—that is, while the train was moving. An operator would attach orders with a string to a pole with a hoop on it and stand trackside with the pole, for the trainmen to grab orders as the train passed at speed. Two sets of orders were handed to trains—one for the headend, one for the rear. This procedure was known as "hooping up orders." In some locations, fixed train order poles were installed, making it unnecessary for operators to stand trackside as the train passed. Instead, the orders would be strung on the fixed poles.

Train order signals, described earlier, indicated when a train needed to collect orders. A clear signal indicated that a train had no orders, a yellow signal indicated that a train needed to slow to take orders on the fly, and a red signal meant a train needed to stop and sign for orders.

In later years, the telephone replaced the telegraph, and by the 1970s, radio began to replace the telephone. Only a few railroads use traditional timetable and train order rules anymore. Today, operating authority is routinely transmitted verbally from dispatcher to train crews by radio, using standardized language (see Chapter 6). Although some radio dispatching systems are comparable to traditional train orders, operating rules have evolved since the days of the telegraph.

BLOCK SIGNALS

The development of block instruments in England by Edward Tyer (who patented an instrument in 1852) and later by Charles E. Spagnoletti and William Preece contributed to the widespread adoption of absolute block signal systems on British railways. In the 1870s, Tyer perfected the electric staff system, which allowed for added safety on single-track lines (see Chapter 3).

The first application of the block system in the United States was installed by Ashbel Welch on the United New Jersey Canal and Railroad Companies, beginning in 1865. Authors Brignano and McCullough indicate that Welch invented his block system independently of similar systems in place on British railways. This conclusion appears improbable, as during this formative time in American railway history there was considerable transatlantic discourse on railway practices. A man of Welch's stature would have been well informed of signaling developments in Britain.

◗ A typical US&S Style-B lower-quadrant block signal used on the Boston & Maine. The top blade is the home signal, designated by a red blade with a pointed end. The bottom blade is a distant signal to the next home signal, designated by yellow blade with a fishtail end. An advantage to the semaphore is that aspects are easily interpreted, even in difficult lighting. This type of signal was standard on the B&M until replaced by color-light and, later, searchlight signals. Brian Solomon

31

The mechanically operated two-position lower-quadrant semaphore was widely used as a block signal in Britain after 1876. This style of signal did not gain popularity in the United States until the 1890s. Note the ornate Victorian finial atop the mast that serves both to decorate the signal and to keep birds from landing on it and fouling the blade. Brian Solomon

In Britain, the two-position upper-quadrant semaphore gained favor in the early twentieth century, but the three-position upper-quadrant semaphore did not. The Barnstaple down-express gets a "clear" (raised diagonal) aspect from a two-position upper-quadrant on the Southern Region at Basingstoke in the spring of 1966. Fred Matthews

While Welch may have independently devised the particulars of his block system, he incorporated elements of British block practice and contemporary maritime communications in his system.

In reaction to serious accidents in Britain during the 1870s and 1880s, the Board of Trade, which oversaw British railway affairs, compelled railways to install absolute block on double-track lines and block-and-staff systems on single-track lines. In 1889, a disastrous accident occurred near Armagh in Ireland that had a dramatic effect on British signaling practices. An excursion train loaded with schoolchildren was being separated to double over a grade when the rear section broke loose and rolled backward out of control, causing a devastating crash with a following passenger train. There were 80 fatalities, mostly children. It was determined that proper signaling and automatic braking could have prevented the dramatic lost of life.

The subsequent public outrage resulted in the 1889 Regulation of Railways Act, which mandated the use of block signals and automatic braking systems on all passenger lines in the United Kingdom. The portion of the first page of the act relating to signals, reprinted in *The Runaway Train—Armagh 1889*, by J. R. L. Currie, reads as follows:

> *Be it enacted by the Queen's most Excellent Majesty, by advice and consent of the Lords Spiritual and Temporal, and Commons, in this present Parliament assembled, and the authority of the same as follows:*

> *1.—(1.) The Board of Trade may from time to time order a railway company to do, within a time limited by the order, and subject to any exceptions or modifications allowed by the order, any of the following things:*

> *(a.) To adopt the block system on all or any of their railways open for the public conveyance of passengers;*

> *(b.) To provide for the interlocking of points and signals on or in connexion with all or any of such railways[.]*

The result of this act was that British railway practice became firmly committed to established signaling practices of the period. As a result, the manual block system with two-position semaphore signaling became the standard in Britain and remained largely unchanged on most lines until the end of the steam era, in the 1960s. By contrast, American railways, unaffected by this act, adopted signaling much later and tended to use more advanced systems. American lines generally chose automatic block systems, which were cheaper to operate and involved more advanced technology, such as track circuitry.

By the early 1890s, most British lines were protected by block signaling, but it would take several more decades before American lines enjoyed the same level of protection. Today, almost 115 years after the 1889 Regulation of Railways Act, some American lines still operate without the benefit of fixed block signaling and instead rely upon verbal authorization of train movements.

Although not universally applied, manual block signaling systems were adopted by some lines in the United States, as were staff systems. One of the best-documented and most extensive examples of the electric staff system was on Southern Pacific's Donner Pass crossing, where the line passed through nearly 40 miles of tunnels and snow sheds.

AUTOMATIC BLOCK DEVELOPMENT

The principle of the space interval had many safety advantages but was costly to implement. American lines were less inclined to install manual block because of the high labor costs the system entailed. It was impractical to implement manual block on many rural lines, where distances were long and traffic relatively light. The development of automatic block signaling allowed technology to provide a space interval less costly than the labor-intensive manual block system. In addition, automatic block had the ability to detect improperly set switches, broken rails, and other defects not protected by manual block.

The track circuit became the most important element in modern American signaling (see Chapter 5). According to Brignano and McCullough, an English patent vaguely describing track circuits was dated to 1848. They also mention another English patent from 1853 that used the rails for communication. In 1860, William Bull was granted an English patent that provided for use of sectional rails to show a train's progress.

The first track circuits were tested in Britain in the 1860s. Richard Blythe, in *Danger Ahead,* explains that W. R. Sykes implemented an experimental track circuit on the Chatham and Dover Railway, in the southeast of England. Sykes' results were inconclusive and unsuccessful, and Blythe indicates that his experience may have in fact soured British impressions of track circuit technology.

Despite early British interest in track circuitry, the first successful application of the track circuit is generally credited to William Robinson, a man of Irish birth, working in America. Brignano and McCullough explain that Robinson started his work in 1867, at a time when railroad safety was becoming a significant public issue. He first worked with models. Then, in 1870, at a fair in New York City,

he publicly demonstrated how a relay-controlled electric track circuit could positively detect a train on a section of track and thus actuate automatic signals.

Robinson, a promoter as well as an inventor, convinced the Philadelphia and Erie—later a component of the Pennsylvania Railroad—to further his experiments on their lines. With the help of P&E, he established the first automatic

Britain's Great Western Railway continued to use two-position lower-quadrant semaphores. More than five decades after nationalization and the subsequent reprivatization of British railways, a few former GWR lines are still so equipped. A class 166 diesel railcar gets a "clear" at Worcester Foregate Street in June 1999. Brian Solomon

signal installation in the United States at Kinzua, in the northwesterly corner of Pennsylvania. For two years he perfected his track circuit system.

Initially he worked with an open-circuit system, but he found that it did not adhere to basic failsafe principles. Failsafe operation is crucial to railway signaling, and systems that have not adhered to failsafe principles have resulted in tragedy. Signaling that does not fail safe may allow the false impression of safety in case of failure, resulting in the problem with the British three-position slotted-mast semaphores discussed earlier. In a failsafe signal system, technical failure of components or other flaws will put a signal in its most safe position. Thus, the system literally fails safe.

The basic open-circuit system exhibited several serious flaws. Electrical failure as a result of low battery power, a broken wire, or outside interference caused signals to display a false "clear" aspect. Also, a signal could indicate a false "clear" in situations where a train either became separated (broke in two) in the block section, leaving part behind, or entered a main track in the middle of a section from a siding or spur.

In response to these problems, Robinson redesigned his track circuit around a closed-circuit principle. Using the closed-circuit system, his signals would automatically display their most restrictive aspects by gravity in case of an electrical failure. In addition, all wheel-axle pairs of a train would act on the circuit, insuring that any pair of wheels would shunt the circuit, causing a signal to display its most restrictive aspect indication.

In 1872, Robinson publicly demonstrated advantages of the closed-circuit system on at fair in Erie, Pennsylvania, and received a United States patent for the closed-track circuit on August 20, 1872. According to Brignano and McCullough, William A. Baldwin, general superintendent of the P&E, encouraged Robinson to install the closed-track circuit at several locations along the railroad.

The success of Robinson's closed-track circuit attracted Pennsylvania Railroad officials. According to the October 16, 1908, issue of *Railway Gazette*, shortly after the circuits were installed, top PRR officials, including Alexander Cassatt, Frank Thompson, and Robert Pitcairn, traveled to inspect Robinson's automatic signaling installations on the P&E. These officials used their influence to encourage further investment in automatic signal development.

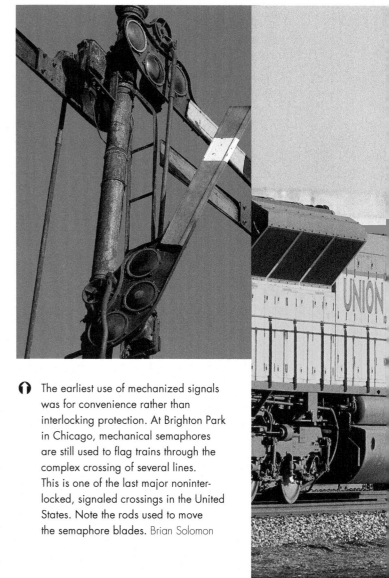

The earliest use of mechanized signals was for convenience rather than interlocking protection. At Brighton Park in Chicago, mechanical semaphores are still used to flag trains through the complex crossing of several lines. This is one of the last major noninterlocked, signaled crossings in the United States. Note the rods used to move the semaphore blades. Brian Solomon

By the end of 1873, Robinson had implemented several more installations on different lines, including the Baltimore & Ohio. From there he moved to Boston, to install pioneering automatic block signal systems. His success led him to form the Union Electric Signal Company, which attracted George Westinghouse—another great pioneer in railway safety known for his famous air brake systems. Impressed with Robinson's track circuit signaling, Westinghouse bought a controlling interest in the Union Electric Signal Company and, about 1881, reorganized it as The Union Switch & Signal Company.

Since that time, US&S has been one the principal American companies involved in the development and application of railway signaling in the United States and many other countries. It is known colloquially among signal engineers as "The Switch."

Robinson wasn't the only one developing automatic block signaling. In Germany, Siemens & Halske had designed a form of basic automatic block, using disc and semaphore signals, by 1875. Perhaps the best known of the early block signals was the automatic enclosed disc signal—popularly known as the "banjo signal," because of

On February 21, 2003, a train led by a Union Pacific SD90MAC on the old Baltimore & Ohio Chicago Terminal had the signal at Brighton Park. This complex, noninterlocked crossing is controlled from the switch shanty near the semaphores. The track in the immediate foreground is the old Pennsylvania Panhandle, which runs parallel to the B&OCT and the former New York Central Chicago Junction, all of which cross the former Alton. Brian Solomon

The Union Switch & Signal Company, of Swissvale, Pennsylvania, is a major supplier of signal hardware and signal system design. This signal equipment box, photographed along the Southern Pacific at Oyster Point, California, dates from the early twentieth century. In later years the "T" was dropped, and such boxes were labeled just "US&S Co., Swissvale, PA."
Brian Solomon

The Hall disc signal was one of the first signals used for automatic block service in the United States and predated the use of the automatic semaphore by a decade. The disc signal, commonly known as a "banjo signal" because of its shape, displayed two aspects. The window in the signal was either clear or displayed a colored cloth disc, as seen here.
Brian Solomon

its distinctive shape—manufactured by the Hall Signal Company.

According to Brignano and McCullough, this company was founded in 1871 by Thomas Seavey Hall, who had invented the characteristic disc signal two years earlier. Although Hall disc signals were used in a variety of applications, including as interlocking signals, as highway grade-crossing protection, and as "take siding" signals, their application as automatic block signals is perhaps most significant.

The signal head consisted of a wooden or metal frame in the shape of an inverted banjo. A circular window revealed the position of the disc, which either filled the window or was hidden from it. The signal frame was designed to protect the mechanism from the weather. The signal mechanism operated a cloth-covered disc mounted on a rod and balanced by a counterweight at the far end.

Silk was often used as the translucent disc covering.

A hole in the signal allowed it to display two aspects: one with the disc, the other without. Control of the disc was by a simple mechanism consisting of a pair of electro-magnetic relay arms: one to move the disc out of the window—the less restrictive position—and the second to hold the disc out of the window. When energized, the second mechanism acted as locking catch, to hold the disc out of sight of the window. When it was de-energized, the catch released, allowing the disc to fall into the more restrictive position, insuring failsafe operation. Any interruption of current, either from a train shunting the track circuit or electrical failure, would automatically result in the signal displaying its most restrictive aspect. The meaning of these aspects varied, depending on how the specific signal was used.

This Hall disc signal may seem strange today, when

B+M TRAIN 3327 - ENGINE 3700 - NORTH WOBURN, MASS.

🎧 An old Union Switch & Signal banner signal was used as a station protection signal on the Boston & Maine at North Woburn, Massachusetts. This photograph was made about 1947, and the banner-type signal was already a relic. The US&S banner closely resembled the Hall disc signal (popularly known as a "banjo"), which dates from roughly the same period. A station protection signal warned of a train stopped at a station on double-track. Donald S. Robinson; H. Bentley Crouch collection

color-lights are standard, but in its day, it would not have seemed unusual. In the early years of signaling, a variety of disc and flag signals had been tried. The Hall disc was similar to banner signals also in use at that time. The disc was lightweight and was easily moved by a relatively inexpensive and reliable electromagnet mechanism. By comparison, a heavy semaphore blade required a more substantial and more complex mechanism, which could neither be cheaply

manufactured nor operated reliably in the 1870s and 1880s.

Hall disc signal aspects did not follow today's standards, adhering more closely to aspects of the period. Since each signal displayed but two aspects, block signals were arranged in pairs, one acting as home signal, the other as a distant signal. (The term "distant signal" was derived from British practice. In American practice, a distant signal was sometimes known as an "approach signal." To avoid confusion with an "approach" aspect, it is important to remember that an "approach signal" is fixed hardware that shows either an "approach" or a "clear" aspect, mimicking the condition of the home signal in front of it.)

In one early Hall configuration, the open hole showed "clear" (corresponding with the traditional "clear" aspect of the time), while a home signal displayed a red disc for "stop" or "danger" (as the "stop" aspect was then called). The distant signal would display "clear" if the home signal was

Boston & Albany 4-4-0 No. 1156 leads the *Albany Flyer* at Dalton, Massachusetts, in 1909. The Boston & Albany was among the first American railroads to embrace signaling on a large scale and used a variety of early hardware. On the left side is a mechanical lower-quadrant semaphore with a wooden mast. Note the counterweights below the blades on the right side of the signal mast. To the right of the train is what appears to be an old Union Switch & Signal banner signal. The Boston & Albany also used Hall Disc signals, although few good photos of these signals exist today.
F. H. Worcester,
Railroad Photographic Club;
Robert A. Buck collection

"clear." If the home signal displayed "stop," the distant would display a blue disc indicating "approach" (then known as "caution"), warning a locomotive engineer that the signal ahead was displaying "stop."

Advanced warning was needed to allow a train time to stop short of a red signal. If a train occupied the block ahead of the home signal, the home signal displayed a red disc and the distant signal a blue one. When the block was clear, both home and distant signals would display "clear" aspects. This system was devised for operation on directional double-track where one train would follow another. Signals were lit with oil lamps for night operation.

Originally, Hall had devised his own system of automatically actuating these signals. The February 13, 1875, issue of *The Railroad Gazette* explains how the system was supposed to work This is an excerpt:

> Much of the apparent complication of the system disap-pear[s] when, on examination, we find that only two instruments are employed for each block section, one to enable the train to close an electric circuit, and the second a signal to show when this circuit has been closed. The first of these, known as the atmospheric track instrument, consists

> of a stout iron level placed just outside the track, so that the wheels of the train passing press down one end and throw the other up. The circuit is thus closed, and to prevent the action from being too instantaneous the lever raises an iron piston which descends by its own weight, but may be held back by a little valve which prevents the air from following it too rapidly, and thus renders its motion quick or slow at will.

Hall signal mechanisms used low-voltage batteries. When a train left one circuit and passed the distant signal in the next section, it moved over similar mechanisms that cleared the signals on the previous block. This created a definite space interval protected by two signals. Hall also provided for an electric circuit used to ring an annunciator bell in a nearby station, warning of an approaching train, and a key-operated switch to allow a stationmaster to manually set signals to "danger."

In later years, Hall signals were used in conjunction with track circuit blocks, which proved more reliable and less complex than Hall's system and other such electro-mechanical means of indicating track occupancy. Hall advertised that its signals normally displayed restrictive

Lower-quadrant signals that showed "clear" with a vertical position were unusual in North American practice, except for the use as train order signals. Here, lower-quadrant signals protect a diamond crossing of the Canadian National and Canadian Pacific at Harriston Junction, Ontario. The lower arm is a fixed marker with a red light, used to distinguish this as an absolute signal. The upper arm is manually operated by levers on the ground. Jim Shaughnessy

indicating the Reading, Michigan Central, and Chicago & North Western. *Railway Gazette* reported in 1908 that by 1904, 4,697 "enclosed disc" signals were working in automatic block service in the United States. The majority of these were Hall's.

In the 1880s, great interest developed in automatic block signaling in the United States. It was seen as the most practical and cost-effective way of providing protection for following trains and safely increasing line capacity. Hall disc signals were popular on some lines but suffered from several disadvantages—notably that they were difficult to see at night and in fog. Another type of signal was Union Switch & Signal's banner clockwork type—which, like the Hall signal, was battery operated and would show two indications.

The Pennsylvania Railroad, which has earned many "firsts" in American signaling practice, was among the earliest lines to adopt semaphores. By the 1870s, PRR was using semaphores for interlocking. In 1882, the Pennsylvania Railroad installed the first electropneumatic lower-quadrant semaphores and two years later was the first to install an automatic block network using electropneumatic semaphores between East Liberty and Wilkinsburg, Pennsylvania. *Railway Gazette* indicated that at the end of 1884, 65 electropneumatic semaphores were in service.

indications rather than clear. Signals were designed to clear ahead of a train, provided the block was unoccupied. This was an added safety feature that required additional circuitry.

Hall's early customers were New England railroads, including the Boston & Lowell, Eastern Railroad, Boston & Albany, and the New York, New Haven & Hartford. By spring 1875, the Boston & Albany, which was then one of the richest and most progressive railways in the United States, had equipped 44 miles of line between Boston and Worcester with Hall disc signals. Later, the use of Halls was extended toward Springfield.

At the same time, the New Haven had proposed to equip its entire line from Boston to New York with Halls. By the early 1900s, many lines were employing Hall signals,

The Union Switch & Signal company perfected this type of signal, which worked using principles similar to the Westinghouse Automatic Airbrake. A compressed-air cylinder acted on rods that pushed the semaphore blade into the less restrictive 45-degree position (which could be used to indicate either clear or caution, depending on whether the signal was a home signal or a distant), while the blade was counterweighted to allow gravity to pull it into its most restrictive horizontal position when air pressure was released. Compressed air from a remote air compressor plant

Failure to obey signals can result in disaster. This head-on collision on Union Pacific at West Junction in Houston, Texas, was photographed on October 25, 1997. It was the result of a train overrunning a red signal. Tom Kline

(operated by a stationary steam engine) fed air into the cylinder, which was regulated by a valve controlled by an electromagnet. When the track circuit was shunted as a result of a train in the block, the electromagnet released the cylinder, allowing the signal to return by gravity to the stop position. As with the Hall disc signal, this practice ensured failsafe operation.

Another innovation was the combining of home and distant signals on a common mast, giving an engineer a clearer picture of line condition. In the typical arrangement, the home signal blade was on top, with the distant signal directly below it. With this pattern, the top blade showed the condition of the block immediately ahead of the signal, while the bottom blade mimicked the condition of the next home signal, giving advanced warning. The top signal used a flat-ended blade, and the bottom one used a "fishtail" blade (an inverted chevron that resembled the tail of a fish).

When both blades were lowered in the 45-degree position, the next two blocks were clear. If the top blade was in the 45-degree position but the bottom blade was in the horizontal position, the immediate block ahead was clear, but the engineer knew to expect to find the next signal indicating "stop." If both blades were in horizontal, the signal indicated stop. Although a twin-blade lower-quadrant semaphore can in theory display four aspects, this basic arrangement had neither provision nor need for a signal to display the top blade in the horizontal position and the bottom blade in the 45-degree position.

For night operation, these signals were lit with oil lamps. In the 45-degree "clear" positions, the lamps would have been viewed directly—that is, with no color—and would have appeared white, giving a "clear" indication consistent with contemporary practice. The home signal would have used a red glass in the horizontal position, while the distant signal used a greenish colored glass in the "caution" position.

Initially, PRR painted its automatic semaphore blades red with white stripes but later changed this, and by the 1880s, the home signal blade was red with a white stripe, while the distant signal was green with a white stripe. This practice was not unique to PRR, and a number of railroads had adopted these colors and shapes for their blades in the early days of the automatic semaphore.

American semaphore practice, although derived from early British practice, exhibited several distinct differences. The first and most obvious difference was signal placement: British double-track railways run on the left, and consequently, engines are run from the left-hand side, so signals, even on single-track lines, are typically located to the left of the track and are also designed to pivot to the left.

In general, traditional American practice was exactly the opposite: trains run on the right, and engines are run from the right so signals are placed on the right and pivot to the right. (There are several notable exceptions to this trend. Some American semaphores, such as "smash board" signals, were deliberately designed to pivot to the left and featured large blades that would strike the front of the locomotive if passed in the stop position. These were usually placed at drawbridges and other places where running through a stop signal would have especially dire consequences. New Haven Railroad also used some semaphores that pivoted to the left. In its electrified territory, it used very short left-pivoting semaphores positioned below the wires. A few of these unusual signals remained in service until the mid-1980s.

Other differences in semaphore blades are more subtle. For reasons that remain a mystery, American semaphore blades took on a longer, more slender character than British semaphores, which tended to be shorter and wider. Also, American blades feature a slight outward taper, whereas British practice normally favored blades with nearly parallel sides.

By the late 1890s, electric motor technology had advanced sufficiently to enable the manufacture of reliable all-electric semaphores, eliminating the need for pneumatic components. This allowed automatic signals to be placed remotely, where pneumatic equipment may not have been cost-effective.

However, the invention of superior signaling technology rarely meant that railroads dispensed with earlier systems—quite the contrary. Obsolete technology was often installed concurrently with the latest innovations. Railroads were notoriously resistant to change, and many lines preferred to standardize the type of equipment they used, thus shunning the rapid adoption of new products.

So, despite the advantages of all-electric semaphores, some lines continued to install electropneumatic semaphores as well as more primitive systems, such as Hall's enclosed disc, while others resisted the use of automatic block signals altogether and continued to rely entirely on older train control systems, such timetables and train orders or manual block. The October 16, 1908, issue of *The Railway Gazette* noted that in 1899, there were 2,263 electropneumatic semaphores and just 204 all-electric semaphores in the United States; five years later, there were an estimated 6,000 electropneumatic semaphores and 6,933 all-electric semaphores. By that time, the all-electric semaphore was clearly the preferred type of signal but had by no means entirely superseded the electropneumatic type.

By 1908, the lower-quadrant all-electric semaphore had become the dominant type of American block signal, *Railway Gazette* noted that more all-electric semaphores had been sold in the previous three years than all automatic signal types over the previous 25 years.

A NEED FOR AUTOMATIC BLOCK

In its basic form, automatic block is primarily designed to protect following movements. It can be used on either single or double-track in conjunction with other forms of control, such as traditional timetable and train order rules, to authorize train movements. Automatic block operations are discussed in Chapter 5.

Following the end of the American Civil War in 1865, railroad traffic grew dramatically. Railroads evolved and, during the latter part of the nineteenth century, trains grew longer and heavier and were being operated at ever faster speeds. This growth strained, and too often compromised, the traditional rules of timetable and train order operation. Greater train weight and faster speeds increased braking distances. Despite the introduction of the Westinghouse Automatic Airbrake in 1872, the potential for disaster had become much greater than in the formative years of the railway.

Despite the development of track circuits and automatic block signals, most railroad companies hesitated to adopt signaling, partly because of the costs of implementation and maintenance. Sadly, by 1900, serious railway accidents had become alarmingly frequent in America. Accidents were caused by a variety of failures: runaway trains, collapsing bridges, and head-on collisions.

One of the most common accidents—and a type easily avoided by proper signaling—was the rear-end collision. Too often, rear-end accidents occurred when a train stopped, failed to properly protect its rear-end, and was struck from behind by a closely following train. Proper rear-end protection was provided for under the rules. If a train slowed and fell behind schedule, it was required to drop colored flares that burned for a designated period to warn following trains of inhibited progress. When a train made an unscheduled stop, a brakeman or flagman was required to run back and provide protection using flags, lanterns, and track torpedoes.

It was common American railroad practice to run a scheduled train in multiple sections when traffic was heavy. Each section was a separate train, consisting of an engine and cars operating on the same timetable authority as the regularly scheduled train. While the safe operation of multiple sections was provided for in the rules, two or more trains often followed each other over a line in rapid succession, running just a few minutes apart and relying on the time interval alone for separation.

Most of the time, trains operated without incident and, when they stopped, had proper protection, but when the rules were overlooked or ignored, crashes were possible. Various factors could occasionally conspire to cause a brakemen to neglect his duty. Fatigue caused by overwork was a problem, and in the days before federal hours-of-service laws, railroads would routinely work men for 20 hours or more without proper rest.

The list of notable rear-end collisions includes a relatively minor disaster on the Illinois Central on April 30, 1900, that killed the engineer of the railroad's express passenger train, the *Cannonball*. The unfortunate engineer was the legendary Casey Jones, a man known for his fast running. Although forgotten today, a far more serious rear-end collision occurred on the Illinois Central at Kentwood, Louisiana, on November 14, 1903, killing 32 people. The

tragedy is that both of these wrecks should have been prevented by automatic block signals. Some railroads, such as the Pennsylvania, Boston & Albany, and New Haven, were early leaders in automatic block protection of their lines.

Automatic block protection was gradually implemented on American lines. According to *Railway Gazette*, by 1915, automatic block signals were protecting 13,408 miles of single-track and 16,281 miles of double-track, for a total of 29,689 route miles. In 1919, *Railway Gazette* reported that the total had risen to 37,969 miles, although it also noted that roughly 48 percent of passenger miles in the U.S.A. remained unprotected. John Armstrong, in his 1957 *TRAINS Magazine* article "All About Signals," reported that 81,300 route miles and 112,000 track miles were protected. Eventually, the majority of American mainlines enjoyed the benefits of ABS signaling, yet to this day, some secondary lines have no ABS protection.

UPPER-QUADRANT SEMAPHORES

Lower-quadrant automatic block semaphores displayed only two aspects. As demonstrated earlier, a signal with two arms was used obtain three aspects. By the early twentieth century, faster trains and more complicated operations in the United States encouraged the development of more complex signaling, which created a need for more signal aspects.

The modern three-position upper-quadrant semaphore was patented in 1903 but was not sold widely until about 1908. By that time, Hall, US&S, and General Railway Signal all sold upper-quadrant semaphores. Upper-quadrant made it easier and cheaper for signals to display more aspects. A single-arm upper-quadrant semaphore could replace a twin-arm lower-quadrant signal in ABS service. The Pennsylvania Railroad applied the upper-quadrant semaphore experimentally, as illustrated by this article from the *Altoona Tribune* of August 30, 1877:

> *The Pennsylvania Railroad Company are about adopting a new mechanical signal board for use in their block signal system, consisting of two horizontal arms, made of*

When technology fails, railroads resort to time-honored practices. In August 1987, an operator temporary stationed at Westfield, Massachusetts, hands orders to an eastbound Conrail freight on the old Boston & Albany route. The newly installed cab signal system had break-in difficulties, forcing Conrail to resort to passing orders to trains by hand. Brian Solomon

iron perforated with large holes to allow the wind to pass through, and erected on a high post just outside the signal tower window. The upper arms governs east bound trains, the lower one west bound trains. When the arm is horizontal, it indicates red or black, (a full stop). When it is elevated at an angle of 45 degrees, it denotes green, which means caution. When the arm is vertical, it indicates white, or a clear track. At night time there are to be colored lights, red, green, and white, which with move with the arm to the different position. One of these experimental signal boards has been placed at Shadyside station.

Modern upper-quadrant semaphores used solid blades, as opposed to the perforated ones tried by PRR. The basic upper-quadrant aspects are basically the same as those described in the article, although the colors used for lamps were modified, as explained later. Upper-quadrant semaphore arm positions were chosen to avoid confusion of aspects with lower-quadrant signals. If a three-position lower-quadrant semaphore were used, the 45-degree aspect could have potentially conflicting interpretations. This aspect indicates "clear" on a two-position lower-quadrant semaphore, while with a three-position lower-quadrant semaphore it would indicate "approach."

While American use of the lower-quadrant semaphore was derived from British practice, the three-position upper-quadrant semaphore was strictly an American innovation. British signal engineers eyed American developments with interest and caution. A few British railways imported the concept of three-position upper-quadrant semaphores, starting during the World War I period, but the practice was not widely adopted in Britain. In 1924, the Institution of Signal Engineers in Britain recommended against the widespread adoption of three-position upper-quadrant semaphores and instead encouraged the use of color-lights for three-position signals. In Britain, the upper-quadrant signal was instead developed as a two-position block signal. Some railways in other countries adopted basic American semaphore practices, including lines in Canada and Australia.

LATER HISTORY

General Railway color lights at Pando, Colorado, on Tennessee Pass in September 1996. In 1928, D&RGW installed GRS color-lights over 72 miles of line between Salida and Minturn, Colorado. Furthermore, the 3 percent eastward ruling grade made Tennessee Pass a serious bottleneck. In the late 1920s, Denver & Rio Grande Western commissioned one of the earliest CTC installations over the pass, to ease operations. The shade over the signal head makes viewing the lights easier in bright sun.
Brian Solomon

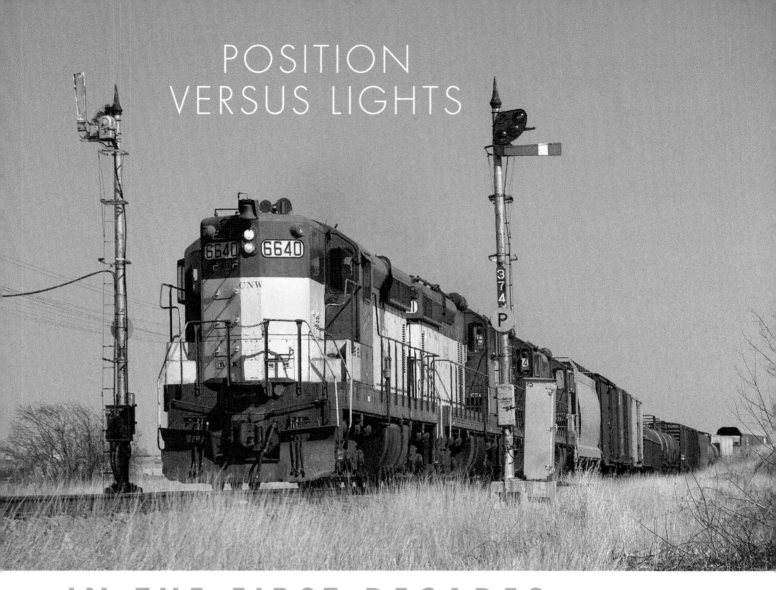

POSITION
VERSUS LIGHTS

IN THE FIRST DECADES of the twentieth century, philosophical differences arose regarding the style of fixed signals. Advocates of traditional semaphores argued for the safety advantages of position-based aspects. The position of the semaphore arm was seen as free from ambiguous interpretation, while color-lights were considered less distinct. Another concern was that color blindness in engineers could lead to misinterpretation of aspects.

Yet the ability to see semaphore blades at night posed problems. Using colored lights was a common solution, but this resulted in a signal effectively having both a day and a night aspect. Creative American inventors devised creative solutions for making semaphore arms more visible at night, such as the use reflective material, attaching lights and lamps to arms, frontal illumination, and even illuminating a screen behind the arm, so it could be viewed in silhouette.

In the days before bright electric lights were available, semaphore lenses were lit with dim oil lamps. These burned night and day but were only bright enough to be visible at night. After 1910, improved incandescent electric lamps made possible the general use of color-light signals bright enough for daylight operations.

On March 24, 1990, Chicago & North Western westbound freight ALSSA (Altoona, Wisconsin, to South St. Paul, Minnesota) passes vintage GRS semaphores west of Hammond, Wisconsin, on the old Omaha Line. C&NW used an unusual style of upper-quadrant semaphore blade. These signals were replaced by the end of 1990. John Leopard

STANDARD ASPECTS

As signal engineers devoted energy to devising failsafe signal systems, some traditional practice came under scrutiny. Among these were the lack of standard aspects and the choice of colors used for signal aspects.

One issue was the traditional use of the white light aspect for a "clear" signal. This violated failsafe practice, because the possibility existed that if a signal lens broke or fell out of position, a restrictive aspect could accidentally be interpreted as "clear." Although the white light "clear" aspect had originated in Britain, it fell out favor there following the Abbots Ripton accident of 1876.

In the last quarter of the nineteenth century, green replaced white as the standard "clear" aspect. According to

Michael A. Vanns in *Signalling in the Age of Steam*, the Great Western Railway presented an exception to this practice. Although GWR had adopted green for "clear" on its passenger lines, it also used a purple aspect for "clear" on its slow lines and lines used exclusively for freight. Presumably this was to allow "clear" signals for different tracks to be easily distinguished at night or in thick fog.

The concern was that an engineer might confuse a "clear" signal on the passenger line for one on the slow line. This was contrary to practice on most British lines, some of which used a purple aspect for "stop" on shunting signals (ground signals used for switching). This was done to distinguish a "stop" indication on a low fixed signal from the red lamp on a hand lantern. If every British railway had an entirely independent operation, such incongruent aspects would have presented only a minor problem. However, since it was common for companies to use each other's lines, contradictory or incongruous signal practices by independent railways could result in collisions.

To solve this problem, in 1893, the Railway Clearing House in Britain recommended the use of just two color aspects on mainlines; green for "clear" and red for all cautionary signals. Since in Britain, "home" and "distant" signals were normally clearly defined by position and other identifiers, such as the fishtail semaphore arm, it was not deemed necessary to provide more than two colors.

In regard to signal aspects, American railroads lagged behind their British counterparts, and some lines continued to use the white aspect for "clear" into the early twentieth century. According to an article in May 1949 *Railway Signaling and Communications* by D. L. Killigrew, in 1894, the American Railway Association's committee on signals made recommendations for standard aspects. Initially they encouraged the use of green for "clear," violet for "caution," and red for "stop." But shortly thereafter they reversed this recommendation and retrenched to the previous standard of white for "clear,", green for "caution," and red for "stop."

Eliminating the white for the "clear" aspect posed problems. One difficulty with colored aspects was the lack of standardized glass colors. One railroad's green might be

Traditionally, the white light was used for "clear." This was changed because of the possibility of a broken lens causing a false "clear" indication or a stray electric light being misinterpreted as a railroad signal lamp. In later years, the lunar-white light was used by some railroads for a "restricting" aspect. Switch lamps such as this one were lit with oil lamps; the lenses were designed to focus the dim light of the flame for greater visibility. Brian Solomon close to yellow, another's would be close to blue. There were concerns about the ability of railroad men to distinguish shades of colored light at night, as well as fears of color blindness.

In 1899, New Haven Railroad was the first to use red, yellow, and green, in the modern arrangement. Killigrew mentions that at the time of New Haven's pioneering application of modern signal aspects, the head of Yale University's Psychological Laboratory, Professor E. W. Scripture, gave a lecture on color blindness and railroad signaling to the New York Railroad Club. This lecture was attended by Alanson B. Houghton of New York's Corning Glass Works, a major manufacturer of railroad signal glass. Inspired by Scripture's talk, Houghton asked the professor to continued his research, and over the next five years, Scripture and Dr. William Churchill advanced the study of colored glass and signal lenses.

Between 1904 and 1908, Churchill furthered his work at Corning Glass, developing different glass colors and lenses specifically for railway signaling applications. The aim was to develop standard color signal aspects that could be clearly distinguished from each other and to develop superior signal lenses that would transmit and focus light more effectively. Through this research, Corning developed distinct shades of green, yellow, and red glass for railroad signal aspects. This work established standard shades and introduced the yellow aspect (sometimes described as amber) for use as approach. Although today yellow seems like a natural color for "approach" (or "caution"), it was rarely used before the Corning study.

Following Corning's findings, standard color aspects were established, using red for "stop," yellow for "approach," and green for "clear." Other aspects were developed too. Bluish white was introduced for a "restricting" aspect.

A General Railway Signal model 2A dwarf signal at North Western Terminal in Chicago. Chicago & North Western used an extensive installation of GRS Model 2A semaphores to protect its Chicago passenger terminal. This disc rotates to display different aspects. It is unusual because it uses a painted semaphore on the disc to indicate that it's a semaphore position type signal. Brian Solomon

(Restricting can be used at interlockings to allow a train to proceed at restricted speed to an occupied track. Restricted speed may be defined as not exceeding 15 mph, being prepared to stop short of a train or obstruction.) This latter color is normally referred to as a lunar aspect, making reference to the moonlike hue. Thus a white aspect went from being seen as one of the least restrictive aspects to one of the most restrictive.

Other colors were still used for more specialized applications. Some American lines, such as New York Central, New Haven, and Illinois Central followed the British practice of using a purple aspect for "stop" in certain dwarf signals.

In 1908, the Railway Signal Association adopted standard color specifications. Standard green, yellow, and red lenses for signaling, corresponding to vertical, diagonal, and horizontal upper-quadrant semaphore positions, allowed for the creation of recommended standard signal aspects by the predecessor of the American Association of Railroads. The use of standardized signal aspects was intended to reduce the potential for confusion in interpreting signals.

Fixed signals were limited to three three-position blades. Prior to this, signals took on varied forms, including the possibility of five-arm lower-quadrant semaphores. A standard three-blade upper-quadrant signal could potentially display as many as 27 different aspects. The great variety of new aspects developed by American railroads all come between the basic "clear" and "stop" aspects. These new aspects were designed to give a locomotive engineer a more detailed understanding of the condition of the line ahead, so he could control his train in the safest yet most efficient manner.

New standard aspects were organized for both traditional route signaling and speed signaling. Although the indication of aspects varied, both route and speed signaling follow logical progressions from least restrictive to most restrictive aspects. The standard speed aspects were for normal speed, medium speed, slow speed, and restricting speed. The definitions of these speeds has varied from railroad to railroad and altered over the years. A more detailed explanation of the differences between route and speed signaling is given in Chapter 4. Later, as railways began

The end of the line for a US&S Style-S upper-quadrant semaphore. In May 1987, Conrail replaced this eastbound block signal along the old Erie Railroad mainline at Rathbone with a triangular position-color-light (see to the right above the semaphore). At the time, the Erie, operated as the Southern Tier by Conrail, was still largely double-track, operating with ABS signals under Rule 251 between River Junction and Binghamton, New York. In the 1990s, Conrail converted much of the route to single-track CTC. Brian Solomon

operating fast passenger trains, the "limited speed" signal was developed.

Railroads did not adopt the new standard aspects immediately. John Armstrong indicated in his article "All About Signals" that by the end of World War I, green had largely replaced white as the standard "clear" aspect. The

Interstate Commerce Commission, which regulated American railroads, eventually banned the white aspect for use as "clear." Although the basic colors were standardized, along with rules for the interpretation of new aspects, the application and meaning of aspects, as well as the style of hardware employed to convey them, varied greatly among companies. As described later in this chapter, some railroads, such as the Pennsylvania Railroad, moved away from using color-lights altogether. Many railroads adapted the new standard aspects to their own practices.

SEMAPHORE ADVANCES

An advantage of upper-quadrant semaphores is that the blade is properly weighted, allowing it to fall naturally to the most restrictive aspect without the need for counterweights. Early electric semaphores used a base-of-mast mechanism to operate the arms. The motor in the signal base moved rods in the mast to control semaphore arm position. Improvements in motor technology allowed for the construction of smaller semaphore mechanisms, which permitted the mechanism to be located at the top of the mast instead of the base.

Base-of-mast-mechanism semaphores have included the Union Switch & Signal "style B" lower-quadrant and "style S" upper-quadrant. Top-of-mast-mechanism semaphores include the US&S "style T" upper-quadrant and General Railway Signal "Model 2A" upper-quadrant signal (although the Model 2A could be constructed as either a base-of-mast or top-of-mast signal).

Although the technology advanced, railroads continued to order, install, and maintain signals of an early developmental period. This was done for several reasons, including the desire to keep the hardware along the lines consistent, to avoid confusing signal maintainers and locomotive engineers, and to minimize the number of parts stocked. Traditional signal hardware was designed for high reliability and long service life.

Despite their obsolescence, operating examples of all the above semaphores could be found in use on American railways as late as 2003. However with the rapid pace of change in modern railroad signaling, it is expected that most semaphores will be replaced in the next few years.

COLOR-LIGHT SIGNALS

The first use of a color-light signal on an American railway dates to 1904—when, according to Brignano and McCullough, limited-distance light signals were first installed in the East Boston Tunnel. A year later, they made their debut on the Long Island Rail Road and in 1906 on the approaches to New York Central's Grand Central Terminal—then being electrified with direct-current third rail.

Many early applications of color-light signals were on underground lines and rapid transit systems, where lights were more practical than semaphores and electricity was readily available to power them. Advances in colored glass and lens technology by Corning Glass, combined with advances in electric light technology, allowed for the production of a bright, reliable light signal that could be clearly seen at a distance in daylight. The concentration of

bulb filaments made lamps brighter. Combined with improvements in high-transmission glass, this gave signal lights much greater range. Also, the use of lens prisms made signals more clearly visible at close range.

According to Killigrew in *Railway Signaling and Communications*, by 1913, color-light signals using doublet lenses could be made with a daylight range of up to 4,000 feet—sufficient distance for use in regular mainline service. The advantages of a color-light signal are that day and night aspects are the same, and the signal has no moving parts, thus reducing maintenance.

Color-light signals were designed to display the same aspects as the night aspects of semaphores. Each color-light head corresponds to a semaphore signal blade. So to display the same aspects as a three-blade semaphore, a three-head color-light signal would be used. Each head is designed to be viewed as a separate grouping, and under normal circumstances, only one light in each head should be lit at any

An empty Somerset coal train passes modern color-light signals near the location of the old BC Tower in Buffalo, New York, on November 7, 1987. Although the triangular-pattern color-light dates from the early 1920s, in the last couple of decades it has become a standard design in new railway signaling installations. Brian Solomon

time. Not all signal heads need to be able to display all three basic colors, so some heads in a grouping may feature only the lights needed. For example, a signal features three heads, of which only the top two need to display green, yellow, and red. Since the bottom head needs to display only a red or yellow light, it has just two lamps.

One of the earliest standard color-light signal formats used multiple lamps in a vertical "traffic light" arrangement. Comparisons between railroad signaling and highway signaling are best avoided, because without lengthy explanations, they can result in greater confusion than clarification. However, a few crucial differences between railway color-lights in a vertical pattern and the common highway traffic light (which, incidentally, evolved from railway practice) need clarification.

On typical American railway signals, the green lamp occupies the highest position on each signal head and the red light the lowest position; while on highway traffic lights, the order is reversed, with red occupying the highest position. Railway color-light lamp orientation is also opposite that used by upper-quadrant semaphores.

One reason for the order of lights on railway color-light signals is a function of lens shades, which are needed to make the lamps more visible in bright sunlight. Since snow or debris could accumulate on the lens shades and block the higher lamps, if the red indication were located on top, it could conceivably be blocked. Following the rules of failsafe practice, red is located at the bottom, although not all railroads adhered to this practice. Several lines have used red on top.

A disadvantage of color-light signals compared with semaphores is that light signals can require substantially more electricity to operate. Another problem with color-light signals is lamp failure. This is overcome by electrical circuits that automatically downgrade a signal to the next more restrictive aspect in the event of a bulb failure. If the green lamp has burned out, the signal is wired to automatically display a yellow instead of a green. Furthermore, if a

Snow accumulation can obscure signal aspects. This signal on the BLS Railway in the Alps at Kandersteg, Switzerland, shows the danger of excessive snow. In standard American practice, the red light is place on the bottom of a color-light head. Also, rules typically state that if a signal is malfunctioning, damaged, or obscured, it must be observed as displaying its most restrictive aspect. Brian Solomon

signal suffers a downgrade because of a bulb failure, it can be wired to downgrade the previous signal, so that a locomotive engineer has time to adjust train speed accordingly and is not suddenly faced with an unexpectedly restrictive signal. If an engineer is anticipating a signal to be green and is prepared to react to yellow but instead finds it at red, he might make an emergency brake application, which could cause a derailment.

Initially, the largest applications of color-light signals were by interurban electric lines and electrified steam rail-

🔊 Changing of the guard: On December 6, 2002, new color-light signals were ready to replace traditional GRS searchlights along the Wisconsin Central route at South Nelsons, Wisconsin (now operated by Canadian National but formerly part of the Soo Line). In 1949, Soo Line installed GRS searchlights on 192 miles of mainline between Waukesha and Spencer, Wisconsin, as part of an APB installation. This system was designed to be upgraded to CTC, and the line was later so equipped.
John Leopard

ways. The Milwaukee Road, which began electrifying its Pacific Extension in 1915, was one of the first American railroads to use a large-scale application of color-light block signals. Other railways that electrified portions of their operations often extended the use of color-light signals to non-electrified lines. Among the early users of color-light signals were the Lackawanna, Nickel Plate Road, Chesapeake & Ohio, Illinois Central, South Shore, Rio Grande, Union Pacific, and Santa Fe.

In 1924, Union Switch & Signal introduced a new color-light arrangement, with the three lights on each head organized in a triangular pattern, allowing for a more compact lighting arrangement. This was listed as US&S Style-TR and used 8 3/8-inch-diameter doublet lenses. Lamps were exchanged from the back of the signal, which was opened with a revolving panel that exposed the housings for all three lamps simultaneously (each lamp had its own housing). Exchanging from the rear was done to avoid the possibility that a single lamp housing might be left open

to the daylight, which could cause the appearance of a falsely lit aspect.

General Railway Signal introduced a triangular-pattern color-light by 1925. New York Central was one of the first railroads to use the GRS triangular color-lights, using them to replace gas-actuated Hall lower-quadrant semaphores on its four-track Water Lever Route mainline between Buffalo and Cleveland. Today, the triangular-pattern color-light signal is one of the most common types of signal head used in the United States.

SEARCHLIGHTS

In 1920, the Hall Switch & Signal Company introduced an important new type of color-light, known as the searchlight signal (sometimes referred to as "target" because of its resemblance to a bullseye). This signal used a single focused lamp for each head, which gave good visibility up to 4,000 feet.

The Hall searchlight blended semaphore and color-light principles in one unit. The use of recently developed optical techniques allowed for a very bright aspect with a relatively low-wattage lamp. The lamp was carefully positioned in a highly polished elliptical reflector that focused the light rays through a colored filter, known as a "roundel," then through a lens that made a narrow beam, which could be transmitted a considerable distance.

According to the February 11, 1921, issue of *Railway Gazette*, a Fresnel lens using a toric formation was used for

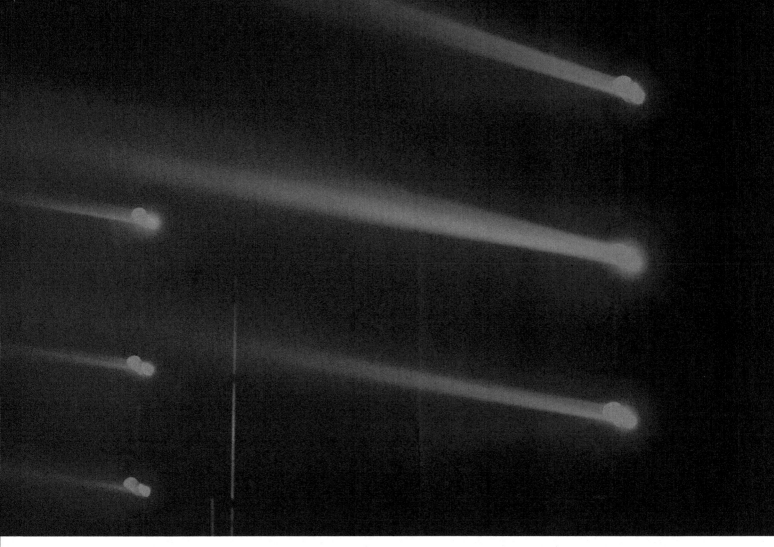

distant applications, while a "Spredlite" lens was used to diffuse the light rays in situations such as a signal on a tight curve, where a broader horizontal field of light was needed. Different aspects were obtained by changing the roundels in front of the bulb with an electric mechanism that was, in effect, a miniature semaphore. *Railway Gazette* explains:

> The coloured 'roundels' are usually about 1 in. in diameter and 1/16 in. thick, and are made of a specially developed heat-resisting glass, ground and polished in accordance with the American Railway Signal Association specifications. As applied for use with alternating current, the 'roundels' are mounted on a moving vane, operated by a polyphase vane relay movement. There are no moving parts other than the vane and its counterweight.

Railway Gazette goes on to explain that the signal mechanism is wired to provide failsafe operation. When the relay is de-energized, the red roundel is displayed; when the current is polarized in one direction, the yellow roundel is displayed; and when polarized in the other, the green

roundel is displayed. Since the arrangement of the roundels features the red in the middle, when the signal clears from yellow to green, the red can be seen briefly.

Because this signal uses just one lamp, it must be so constructed as to account for the possibility of failure. *Railway Gazette* details this:

> The electric lamp used is furnished with a special form of concentrated filament, and is usually provided with two filaments looped one within the other but both located at the focal point of the reflector. One filament has double the life of the other, and is of a lower candle-power. The secondary filament may placed in multiple with the main filament, or may controlled through a cut-in relay which will cause it to light should the main filament burnout.

By use of this double filament, a searchlight will appear abnormally dim when the main filament has burned out, but the signal will not appear totally dark and can continue to function while alerting railway men of its failure. An engineer who passes a dim signal would be required to

Far left: Searchlight signals use a highly focused light beam to make aspects appear bright at great distances with relatively low-wattage lamps. These searchlights on the former Milwaukee Road mainline protect the diamond with the former Soo Line crossing at Duplainville, Wisconsin. On this evening in 1996, a dense fog has made the searchlight beam clearly visible. All signals show red for "stop." Brian Solomon

Union Switch & Signal searchlights protect the east switch at Sais, New Mexico, along the Santa Fe. Compound lenses allow a searchlight to be visible both close up and at a distance. Brian Solomon

report it, so that a signal maintainer could be dispatched to make repairs. In the 1920s, a long-range searchlight would be equipped with a 10-watt bulb, while a short-range signal could operate safely with just a 3-watt bulb. Compare this to the average incandescent bulb use in a home, which is typically in the 40- to 100-watt range.

New York Central was among the first American lines to use Hall searchlights in large-scale installations, using them to replace semaphores on portions of its Water Level Route east of Buffalo, New York. It is interesting that Central was simultaneously installing triangular pattern color-lights west of Buffalo and Hall searchlights east of Buffalo.

Union Switch & Signal bought Hall in 1925, partly to acquire the searchlight patent. By this time, Hall had sold many searchlights to both domestic and foreign railways. Within a year of their introduction, the London & South Western Railway had installed Hall searchlights experimentally. Searchlights found limited application in Britain and Ireland but did not become as popular as other types of color-light signals. By contrast, the searchlight type became the dominant modern signal in America during the middle part of the twentieth century.

The searchlight provides an especially bright aspect favored by many railways. It was manufactured in variations both by US&S and General Railway Signal, the two primary American signal equipment suppliers for many years. The searchlight supplanted the upper-quadrant semaphore as the modern symbol of safety, and tens of thousands were installed on lines throughout North America. By the 1970s, many routes were governed exclusively by searchlights.

The type fell out of favor in the 1980s, when advances in other types of color-lights made them preferable for new installations. The flaw with the basic searchlight is that it still features a moving component, which requires greater maintenance and may be more likely to fail. As of 2003, the searchlight remains a common type of signal head, but its numbers are dwindling rapidly as railroads replace them with modern color-light heads.

POSITION-LIGHT SIGNALS

During the early years of the twentieth century, there was great debate over the virtues and defects of different varieties of signal hardware. Color-light signals were developed as a solution to the problem of day and night aspects, but some signal engineers argued that position signals offered greater safety than color-lights.

Arthur Holley Rudd was a leading signal engineer with the Pennsylvania Railroad and among the most influential men in the field of signal engineering. He came from a distinguished family, studied at Yale University, had worked for a variety of American railway companies, and was one of the earliest American members of the esteemed Institution of Railway Signal Engineers, based in Britain.

During the first half of the twentieth century, the Pennsylvania Railroad was America's foremost railway

Norfolk & Western adopted a position-light system similar to the Pennsylvania's but adopted a few varying practices. N&W used a bottom marker light to indicate an absolute stop. This was exactly the opposite of the PRR, which used a bottom marker light to show a "stop and proceed" aspect, Rule 291. In later years, N&W adopted red lights for "stop" aspects. This view of two "stop" aspects was made at Abbington, Virginia, on March 20, 1991. Tom Kline

company and one of the most progressive in the field of signal engineering, application, and development. But the PRR was known for its individualistic approach to technological development and tended to do things its own way, as demonstrated by its distinctive fleet of steam locomotives. The PRR was the self-proclaimed "Standard Railroad of the World"—a moniker designed to reflect the company's early standardization of locomotive components. PRR took pride in setting industry standards rather than embracing standards established by other authorities.

The rapid development of electric light signals intrigued the PRR officers. Rather than embrace the color-light, Rudd worked with Corning Glass to develop a practical position-light signal. His concept was a signal that displayed aspects using an orientation of the lights rather than the color-lights. The advantage to Rudd's position-light was that the signal provided the same aspects day and night while eliminating the need for moving parts. It was cheaper to maintain than a semaphore while offering greater safety than other types of signals.

With the help of Corning's Dr. William Churchill, Rudd devised a bulb housing that provided a bright light yet minimized the effects of stray light, to avoid the dangers of a false aspect. This housing used a reflector behind the 5-watt bulb to concentrate the light forward and, as in the case of the searchlight described earlier, make it clearly visible at great distances. A conical, egg-like glass, which made the lights appear yellow, protected the lamp and deflected stray light from the reflector. Position-light signals feature very bright aspects as viewed from the position of a locomotive engineer but are deliberately difficult to see if viewed from a sharp angle.

Rudd's first position-lights were installed along the Pennsylvania Railroad's famous Main Line in 1915, on a 15-mile section just west of company headquarters in Philadelphia, between Overbrook and Paoli. These signals were installed in conjunction with PRR's 11,000-volt AC overhead electrification of the line and featured large background shields to protect the view of the signal from the effects of harsh backlight. The aspects mimicked those of upper-quadrant semaphores by using rows of four lamps.

After a few years of service, the position-lights were deemed successful. They pleased locomotive engineers by being easy to interpret and railroad officials for being cheaper to maintain than semaphores. Before PRR adopted the signal for widespread application, they refined the form of the position-light signal head. Each head used rows of three lights oriented around a common center lamp, with the outer lamps forming a circle. Lamps were mounted on bars, with a circular background panel affixed behind the lamps, and shades to prevent backlighting.

Traditionally, this panel was made of Armco iron, measuring 4 feet, 4 inches in diameter, with 7 3/4-inch holes punched in it for the lamps. Each single head can display several basic aspects: "clear," represented by three

The position-light signal had several advantages: its aspects were the same day and night; the bright, focused yellow lights were visible in all types of light; aspects were unlikely to be confused with stray lights; and two heads could be used to display all aspects. This signal, along the former Pennsylvania Railroad at CP Muncy, near Montgomery, Pennsylvania, is displaying "clear." Brian Solomon

vertical lights; "approach," by diagonal lights at a 45-degree angle running from the 1:30 clock position to the 7:30 position; "restricting," by diagonal lights at a 45-degree angle running from the 10:30 position to the 4:30 position; and "stop" (or "stop and proceed") by three lights running horizontally.

An individual signal head is provided with lamps only for the aspects it is expected to display, with unnecessary holes covered over. The lower of two heads uses a slightly different shape for the shield panel. This reflected the

Pennsylvania Railroad
STANDARD SIGNAL ASPECTS–CIRCA 1941

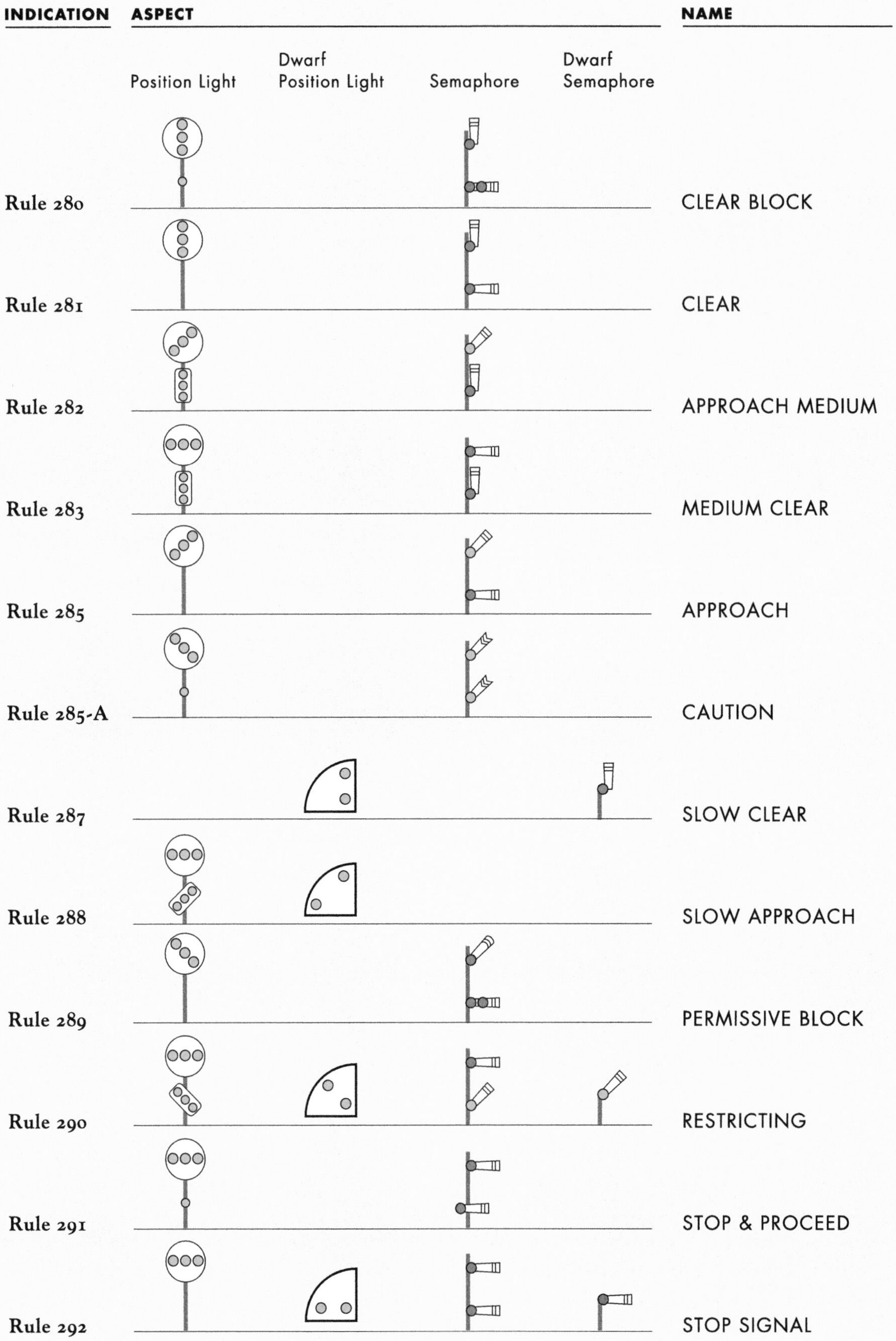

INDICATION	ASPECT				NAME
	Position Light	Dwarf Position Light	Semaphore	Dwarf Semaphore	
Rule 280					CLEAR BLOCK
Rule 281					CLEAR
Rule 282					APPROACH MEDIUM
Rule 283					MEDIUM CLEAR
Rule 285					APPROACH
Rule 285-A					CAUTION
Rule 287					SLOW CLEAR
Rule 288					SLOW APPROACH
Rule 289					PERMISSIVE BLOCK
Rule 290					RESTRICTING
Rule 291					STOP & PROCEED
Rule 292					STOP SIGNAL

DIAGRAM 2.1

Diarmaid Collins / Rochelle Schultz

nature of the lower head, which did not need to display the equivalent of a "stop" signal in PRR's rulebook and would need to display only the diagonal or vertical rows of lights. By using two heads, a great variety of speed signal aspects, mimicking those of two- and three-head semaphores, is possible. Slow speed aspects are provided for by dwarf position signals, which use a different light pattern. These signals are rectangular and use pairs of lights rather than rows of three. To avoid confusion with high signals, the dwarfs use lunar white lamps rather than yellow ones.

Rudd's position-light is a clever design that incorporates many safety features. For example, if one lamp burns out, an engineer can still read the aspect using the remaining two lamps without any risk of misinterpreting the signal. The distinctive spacing and patterns of the various aspects are unlikely to result in misreading an aspect or to produce a "false clear" signal. Also, the aspects are unlikely to be mimicked by other lights unrelated to railway operations. The use of semaphore aspects made it easy for enginemen to interpret the signals while minimizing the potential confusion of aspects between the two types of signal hardware.

From the 1920s onward, the Pennsylvania Railroad installed position-lights as its standard signal type, gradually replacing semaphores and other signals. Union Switch & Signal provided hardware. Some of Pennsylvania's affiliated lines, notably the Long Island Rail Road and Norfolk & Western, also adopted the basic principles of the position-light.

The signal had a slightly different evolution on Norfolk & Western, and aspects varied from those used by PRR. For example Norfolk & Western position-light signals use a single light below the main head to help distinguish absolute signals from permissive "stop and proceed" signals. This is contrary to PRR practice, which used a single dot with a "stop" aspect to give a "stop and proceed" indication.

Even on PRR lines, the basic position-light system underwent evolutionary changes over the years to add greater safety protection and make provisions for new standard aspects. After about 1950, the "stop" aspects were sometimes given added clarity by use of red lights on the outer two positions, while the center light was wired to appear dark. Flashing aspects were added for limited speed indications (which could also be displayed by the addition of a fixed yellow triangular plate that upgraded a medium speed aspect to limited speed).

Amtrak, which operates portions of the former PRR New York, – Philadelphia, – Washington D.C. route, has adapted the PRR system with the addition of more colored lights, making for what is known as "position color-lights." Position-light hardware can still be found along some former PRR lines, now variously operated by Norfolk Southern, Amtrak, and local commuter agencies.

However, in recent years, efforts have been made toward standardizing railroad rulebooks and reducing the number of signal aspects with which crews must be familiar, so this style of signal has fallen out of favor. On many former PRR lines, position-lights are now being phased out and replaced with standard color-light signals. They are still used on the Long Island Railroad and, to a lesser extent, on former Norfolk & Western lines.

The back of a position-light signal on the former Pennsylvania Railroad at New Florence, Pennsylvania. This signal includes a "C" light used in cab signal territory. The "C" light is lit to allow trains without cab signals to proceed to the next interlocking, but they must be prepared to stop at the next home signal. Patrick Yough

COLOR-POSITION-LIGHT

Concurrent with Rudd's development of the position-light was Frank Patenall's invention of the color-position-light for Baltimore & Ohio. Patenall was an Englishman who immigrated to America in 1885. He had worked on signaling in Britain and was an employee of Union Switch & Signal before going to work for B&O in 1891. His earlier achievements included the design of the upper-quadrant semaphore with L. F. Loree, which they jointly patented in 1903, and the development of approach lighted signals.

Paternall's color-position-light uses many of the same principles of the position-light type described above but features a unique way of displaying aspects. This signal combines the position and the color of lights in the display of aspects, to minimize the potential of misreading.

Another defining feature is the use of a single head—which, combined with marker lights, can display as many as 29 different aspects. Using marker lights, the four basic aspects—"clear," "approach," "restricting," and "stop"—can

Color-position-light dwarf signals can display all the aspects high signals can. This dwarf at the Bailey Wye in Baltimore, Maryland, displays "approach." Brian Solomon

be modified for speed signaling. The marker light can occupy any of six positions (top left, top center, top right, and bottom left, bottom center, bottom right) as well as being unlit. The marker light uses either yellow or lunar white, depending on its position. Although the color-position-light may seem awkward and confusing, it was designed with simplicity in mind. An article by Patenall in the July 1925 issue of *Railway Signaling* explained the theory of the color-position-light. Patenall says:

> *The basic arguments in favor of the system are:*
> *1) The day and night indications are the same.*
> *2) With aspects indicating at slow speed, proceed at restricted speed, or proceed, no red lights are displayed; therefore this obviates the necessity of disregarding a stop indication as displayed in conjunction with a proceed indication in [Baltimore & Ohio's] present practice.*
> *3) Instead of trainmen being required to learn 135 diagrams, they will only be required to commit to mind 14 aspects and 6 rules.*
> *4) White upper and lower route markers for high speed and restricted speed routes respectively, indicate clearly which route is set, in conjunction with the block indications displayed.*
> *5) Reduction in the cost of construction, maintenance and operation.*

Another benefit of the color-position-light system is that a dwarf signal is capable of displaying all of the same aspects as a tall signal. Although the color-position-light system was originally designed to display just 14 aspects, a number of additional aspects were later developed. Over the years, B&O and its successors altered and adapted the aspects displayed by these signals. The August 1, 2001, *CSX Transportation Signal Aspect and Indication Rules* guide lists 22 aspects displayed by color-position-light signals. For a better understanding of this unique signaling system's aspects, see Diagram 2.1

COLOR POSITION
Light Aspects

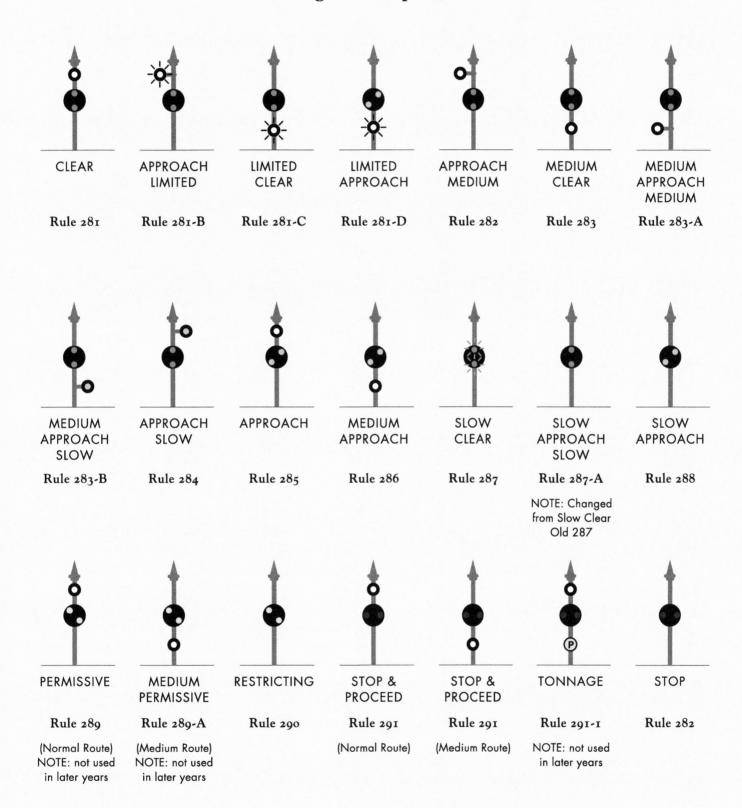

DIAGRAM 2.2

Diarmaid Collins / Rochelle Schultz

➜ Baltimore & Ohio's Staten Island Rapid Transit affiliate was among the first lines to adopt the color-position-light signal. An SIRT train is seen at New Dorp station on August 14, 1959. Note the four-quadrant grade-crossing gates. Richard Jay Solomon

Baltimore & Ohio first installed the color-position-light signal between Deshler and Hamler, Ohio. In the December 1924 issue of *Railway Signaling,* B&O announced that it had ordered equipement for 77 color-position-light signals for an extensive installation on its Staten Island Rapid Transit. Early installations were manufactured by Hall, and later US&S and GRS supplied hardware to B&O. Gradually, color-position-lights superseded most other types of signal hardware on B&O's lines. However, a few semaphore installations remained on old B&O lines through the late 1990s, which were by that time operated by B&O's corporate successor, CSX.

Color-position-lights were installed on other B&O affiliates, including Chicago & Alton, Baltimore & Ohio Chicago Terminal, and Washington Union Terminal Company. Interestingly, the Alton Route was later operated by Illinois Central, Southern Pacific, and finally Union Pacific, which continued to use color-position-light signals. In later years, route aspects were assigned to the traditional hardware.

As with the case of the PRR-style position-lights, the color-position-light style has fallen out favor and is now gradually being replaced with standardized color-light hardware.

Position-lights and color-position-light systems have also been developed by railways overseas. The German railway, DBAG, has extensive installations of color-position-lights along its lines.

ABSOLUTE PERMISSIVE BLOCK AND CENTRALIZED TRAFFIC CONTROL

The General Railway Signal Company was formed in 1904 from the combination of the Pneumatic Signal Company and the Buffalo, New York–based Taylor Signal Company. General Railway Signal (GRS) was a Rochester, New York–based company, located along the New York Central Water Level Route near Lincoln Park, a few miles west of downtown. This company played a significant role in the advancement of railway signaling during the twentieth century, and was a primary supplier of signal hardware. Today, GRS is a component of Alstom and remains an active supplier of railway and transit signaling systems.

According to GRS literature, in 1911, Sedgwick N. Wight, one of the company's signal engineers, developed the Absolute Permissive Block system (APB). This was an advanced type of automatic block signaling, used to increase the capacity of a single-track mainline by allowing greater protection for opposing moves without sacrificing track capacity for following moves. This gives APB a distinct advantage over conventional automatic block systems. APB was especially popular on single-track railway lines in the midwestern United States, where single-track lines were used to handle relatively heavy traffic. The technology that made APB possible was advanced and complex relay installations that could be used to communicate information and detect the direction of traffic.

Sixteen years after the introduction of APB, GRS debuted another of Wight's inventions, which was an even more significant signal system innovation. This was Centralized Traffic Control (CTC), which combines elements of interlocking and automatic block signaling. It allows one operator complete control over a section of line, dispensing with need for timetable and train order operation. The very first CTC installation was put into operation on the Ohio Division of the New York Central, between Stanley and Berwick, Ohio, on July 25, 1927.

Centralized Traffic Control uses technology to supplant traditional railroad rules and allows trains to proceed on the authority of signal indication. Strictly speaking, CTC provides an operator direct control of signals, even those located at great distance, insuring interlocking protection. In actual practice, CTC often also gives an operator remote control of power switches. In effect, a train dispatcher can directly control the movement of trains. This superseded traditional timetable operation and the need to issue train orders through a telegraph or telephone to operators, who would relay them to trains. With the development of CTC, a dispatcher could do the job of many operators from a single centralized electric console. Details of CTC operation are discussed in Chapter 6.

Centralized Traffic Control was one of the most important developments in modern American railway history. In combination with other technological innovations, CTC increased track capacity and improved safety, by reducing the chance for human error, while reducing the number of people required to move trains over the road. Although expensive to install, CTC offered railroads increased

General Railway Signal was one of the primary suppliers of signal hardware and signaling systems to American railroads. It was formed in 1904 from a merger between the Pneumatic Signal Company of Rochester, New York, and the Taylor Signal Company of Buffalo, New York. GRS's traditional company offices were located adjacent to the New York Central Water Level Route, near Lincoln Park in Rochester. Today, GRS is a component of Alstom, one of the leading suppliers of railway equipment in the world. Brian Solomon

flexibility, smoother operations, and lower long-term costs.

GRS invented Centralized Traffic Control, but Union Switch & Signal was quick to promote and improve the system. Just a year after GRS's first CTC installation, US&S applied CTC principles to the Pere Marquette route (later part of the Chesapeake & Ohio, a component of present day CSX), between Bridgeport and Mt. Morris, Michigan.

In 1929, less than two years after the first CTC installation, both GRS and US&S installed all-relay CTC installations. GRS provided the Burlington with a remote-controlled relay interlocking at Lincoln, Nebraska, while US&S installed an all-relay CTC system on the Boston & Maine at Eagle Bridge, New York.

Early CTC installations were typically short stretches of 20 to 30 miles. During the 1930s, US&S developed relay pulse-code systems that allowed two- and three-wire

An Amtrak train passes a color-position-light displaying "approach" on the old Alton, between Chicago and Springfield, Illinois. Brian Solomon

networks to do the work of many traditional circuits, which made more extensive CTC networks practical. GRS also continued to innovate and in 1937 introduced a pushbutton automatic route selection system named the "NX," which stood for "eNtrance-eXit." Interestingly, this system debuted in Brunswick, England, with the first American installation at Girard, Ohio, on the New York Central. In the 75 years since its introduction, CTC has become the dominant form of train control and is now in operation on the majority of

North American mainlines. For many years, CTC operation symbolized progress on American railroads.

Relay circuits are a key component of CTC signaling. These circuits can be extremely complex, involving banks of relays communicating with one another over great distances, using coded pulses. By the early 1940s, both GRS and US&S were selling relay pulse-code CTC systems. The CTC machine is a predecessor of the earliest computers, which were invented independently during World War II by American and British scientists for code breaking.

Subsequent advances in electronic technology have gradually resulted in ever more sophisticated electronics being employed for railway signal control. While many of the basic principles of signaling have remained the same, component size has shrunk, while the amount of control given to a single person has greatly expanded. CTC allowed railroads to close towers, manual block stations, and train order stations. It permitted fewer people to do more work while freeing up track space or permitting the reduction in the number of tracks needed to move trains. Microelectronics and modern communication systems allowed railroads to gradually consolidate their dispatching centers while expanding the territory over which an individual dispatcher desk has authority.

In the four decades following World War II, many mainlines, especially those in the eastern states, suffered from a dramatic loss of traffic. First, passenger traffic declined. From the late 1950s to the late 1960s, railroads cut many passenger trains and drastically trimmed their passenger fleets. In 1971, Amtrak assumed most remaining intercity services, often limited to just one daily run. On many lines, passenger trains disappeared altogether. Local freights, which at one time could be found switching cars in small yards all over the industrial East, gradually became fewer in number as industry declined and railroads switched traffic to intermodal services (either piggyback trailers or containerized shipments).

Some types of traditional traffic dried up as businesses moved, closed shop, or shifted to other transport modes. Perishable traffic, consisting of carloads of fruit and vegetables from the Far West and Florida moving to large eastern markets, was big business for railroads in the steam era. By the late 1970s, much of this traffic was no longer moving on the rails. Likewise, milk traffic disappeared. By the mid-1960s, many railroads were finding that their once busy double-track lines were handling only a few trains a day. The remaining freight traffic was often moved on much longer and heavier trains, made possible by the development of powerful diesel locomotives. Changing traffic patterns placed new demands on signaling but often also left railroads with far more complex signaling systems than they needed.

Declining traffic and falling revenue made railroad management anxious to find ways to reduce operating costs. The installation of CTC provided an ideal solution. CTC, which had enabled railroads to boost capacity of single-track lines during the boom years of World War II, could also be used to trim physical plant and eliminate employees. Many lines converted their double-track mainlines to single-track CTC operation. In theory, fewer mainline tracks required less maintenance, and therefore smaller track maintenance forces. Railroads could close towers by integrating their interlocking functions to centralized dispatching offices. A side benefit was that lifting one track allowed railroads greater access to the existing track, making highway-based maintenance easier.

All across the eastern and midwestern states, scarred rights-of-way and new searchlight signals were the symbol of progress afforded by CTC. Traditional signaling installa-

tions, such as automatic block semaphores, interlocking towers, block offices, and multiple-tier telegraph lines, disappeared.

The downside to this progress was that it contributed to the dehumanizing of the American railroad. CTC allowed railroads to replace people with relays and, later, transistors and microprocessors. While this may have lowered operat-

Color-position-lights on CSX's Mountain Subdivision near West End Tower, West Virginia. The signal on the left displays "stop"; the signal on the right displays "clear." With the B&O system, a "clear" can be displayed only with a white marker light above the pair of vertical green lights. This type of signal should be clearly visible from a distance of 4,000 to 6,000 feet. The grade-crossing gates and flashers are operated by a separate track circuit and are not interlocked with the color-position-lights. Brian Solomon

ing costs and improved the safety of train operations, it did not always result in faster operations. However, because passenger traffic was largely gone, the few delays that might be incurred while trains waited on sidings for meets was only a minor concern.

Boston & Maine is an example. In the late 1920s, B&M was among the first railroads to install CTC, using short, double-track CTC segments with controlled center sidings to provide greater flexibility. At that time it operated a great number of intercity and suburban passenger trains as well as dense freight traffic. Looking at one section, in 1929, B&M commissioned a 13.5-mile section of double-track CTC on its Stony Brook Branch, between Ayer and North Chelmsford, Massachusetts. This line was a bottle-

Some modern signals now use clusters of light-emitting diodes (LEDs) to give signal aspects. This dwarf signal is used north of Chicago's Union Station. Notice that the signal has many LEDs. The head contains LEDs of three colors, one for each aspect. As of this writing in 2003, LED signals are a relatively unusual innovation in American railroad signal practice. Brian Solomon

neck for freight traffic and carried a fair amount of seasonal passenger traffic. At times of peak traffic, this route moved as many as 50 freight and passenger trains daily. Double-track CTC controlled from North Chelmsford allowed the B&M to move traffic fluidly over this line.

After World War II, B&M gradually consolidated control by combining CTC desks and closing towers. Then, as traffic declined, it reduced capacity by single-tracking its mainlines in the 1950s and 1960s, then trimming the number and length of sidings. Today, former B&M lines still feature complex CTC signaling, even though its mainlines carry far fewer trains than they once did.

MEGAMERGERS AND DISPATCHER CONSOLIDATION

Traditionally, dispatching offices were local to a railroad division and might contain only one or two desks. As railroads merged, the trend was toward consolidation, which affected train dispatching and other elements of railroad signaling. First, regional dispatching offices were created by combining smaller local CTC desks. A regional office might contain a half-dozen desks.

Then, as massive freight railroads were created between the 1970s and 1990s, they implemented large-scale dispatcher consolidation, resulting in massive modern dispatching centers. This was made possible by improvements in technology, such as computer-aided dispatching tools, which allowed a single dispatcher to control more territory. Railroads looked to achieve further savings by cross-training dispatchers to cover several desks.

Since the 1960s, the railroad industry been altered by complicated, multifaceted consolidation through numerous mergers, line abandonment, short line spin offs, and other changes. So by the mid-1990s, several massive railroads accounted for the majority of mainline operations in North America. In 1988, CSX was the first major railroad to centralize all its dispatching from one center, in Jacksonville, Florida. Until CSX inherited part of the Conrail system in 1999, nearly all its train dispatching was performed from this location.

The great diversity of signal hardware that existed through much of the twentieth century was a result of the individual practices of the many independent railroads. Signal systems, like steam locomotive design, varied considerably from railroad to railroad; no other country in the world featured such variety in signal practice. The durability of signal hardware and the high cost of replacement had allowed antique systems to continue to function largely unchanged for decades. Some traditional steam-era signal hardware, such as semaphores, has been undergoing a prolonged period of replacement since before World War II, and a few of these signals are still in service. Likewise, PRR position-lights and Baltimore & Ohio color-position-lights—some installed when steam still ruled the railroads and Pullman sleepers were a preferred mode of intercity travel—still display their distinctive aspects to modern freight trains.

However, megamergers and modern technology are altering the face of line-side signaling. In recent times, railroads have consolidated rulebooks and made efforts toward streamlining and standardizing signal systems and signal hardware. All across the United States older, nonstandard hardware is being phased out and replaced with modern equipment. Even the common searchlight signal, once the symbol of modern railroading, has fallen out of favor. Searchlights are now being replaced on a large scale, and will someday be as scarce as the semaphore is today.

Most American railroads now prefer color-light signals. The two most common color-light patterns are the vertical "traffic light" configuration and the three-light triangular configuration. Some lines are installing signals lit by fiber-optic cables or light emitting diodes (LEDs) rather than incandescent lamps, which can be made much brighter than traditional color-light signals.

Modern signals have other distinct advantages over traditional hardware. Because they use no moving parts, they require less maintenance and less frequent inspections and are therefore less expensive to operate and maintain. Modern signal control systems, such as Electro Code 5, control signal aspects directly. They send code through the rail and solid-state interfaces, which is different from older systems that sent coded signals through line wires to activate banks of line-side control relays.

Older signal hardware is often incompatible with modern control systems or incurs significant cost to enable compatibility, making older signals undesirable, despite their historic durability. As railroads modernize their signal systems, they are replacing old signals with new, taking down line wires, and lengthening blocks to better suit modern operating practices.

Baltimore & Ohio's single-track mainline from Grafton to Parkersburg, West Virginia, was equipped with CTC using color-position-lights in the late 1920s. At that time, this was a busy section of track. By the 1980s, traffic had dried up or was diverted, and the line was cut west of Clarksburg and abandoned. This view was made near the end of track in October 1994; the B&O signals were still intact. Brian Solomon

MANUAL BLOCK

The staff system is used on single-track lines under control of manual block, to ensure absolute protection. Only one staff may be issued at a time for each block, and a train must possess the staff to enter the block. This view at the preserved East Lancashire Railway at Ramsbottom Station, England, depicts the time-honored practice of the signalman passing the staff to the locomotive driver while the train is moving. The staff is actually a token attached to a hoop, to make it easier to catch.
Brian Solomon

AS RAILWAYS BEGAN to operate more trains at higher speeds, the system of timetable operation demonstrated inadequacies. In theory, a timetable provided rules for operation that afforded flexibility and guaranteed sufficient safety protection, provided the rules were strictly adhered to at all times. However, as any railway observer is well aware, trains all too frequently fall behind schedule. As trains become delayed, a simple timetable system loses its effectiveness; the efficient movement of trains is impaired, and safety can be sacrificed.

By the 1840s, the electric telegraph had permitted the implementation of practical space interval protection, known as a block system. In a basic block signal system, a line is divided into distinct sections of fixed length, called blocks. Fixed signals are used to strictly regulate the blocks, so as to provide trains with a definite space separation, regardless of the travel speed.

A number of variations on the block system evolved over the years, with differing levels of complexity. Traditional manual block systems require direct intervention to either set signals or grant authority, by issuing a staff, token, or written form. "Automatic block" systems, which automatically actuated signals to govern blocks without any manual intervention, evolved later. These systems are discussed in Chapter 5.

Chapter 1 discussed the development of manual block systems in Great Britain and the United States. Since these systems developed at different times, they evolved with different operational characteristics but retain numerous similarities. Elements of both types are detailed here.

Traditional manual block fell out of favor in the United States with the development of practical automatic block systems, yet some railroads still use manual block systems today. Manual block operation remains common in the British Isles and in many other parts of the world, especially in former British colonies. Understanding manual block provides insights to later types of train control. The mechanics have evolved, but the principles remain the same.

An operator stands ready to hand up orders to a westbound Nickel Plate Road freight led by Berkshire type No. 772 at North East, Pennsylvania. In the United States, timetable and train order rules authorized operations on many lines.
Jim Shaughnessy

BASICS OF MANUAL BLOCK

The basic principle of manual block involves the segmentation of a railway mainline. Blocks are established along the line, with a designated block station situated everyplace where a block ends and another begins. Block length varies greatly and can be anything from a few hundred feet to many miles long, depending on traffic and other operational considerations.

The amount of traffic over a line, train speed, train weight, grades, and the number of mainline tracks all affect block length. A double-track line in level territory with relatively light traffic might use blocks 10 miles long, while a heavily used single-track mountain railway might feature a succession of very short blocks. On a double-track line, each mainline track has its own designated blocks.

One advantage of a manual block system is that new block stations can easily be opened or closed as traffic fluctuates. If traffic is seasonal or is heavy only during part of the day, block stations can be "switched out," to reduce operational costs without substantially altering the rules of operation. A primary disadvantage of manual block is the high amount of labor required. With traditional operations, every open block station required an operator. Some modern systems now work using radio and other remote control systems. These are discussed under Radio Dispatching in Chapter 6.

The basic block system was developed primarily to reduce the risk of accident but also to increase line capacity where block stations are closely spaced, ensuring safe operations on short headways. Initially, manual block was not intended to supersede railway timetable authority but to supplement schedules while providing an added measure of safety. For this reason, in many situations, manual block signals are not intended to authorize train movements but to offer protection to trains. Authority to occupy track is granted by other means: written authorization, timetable, train order, clearance form, staff, or token.

A simple double-track manual block system is the easiest to understand, because in general, trains all move in one direction; therefore, the blocks are used only to protect against *following* movements. With this arrangement, trains are passed from block station to block station in a relay fashion.

Block signals are manually controlled by signalmen and, in accordance with later practice, are normally kept in the "stop" position. Signals are set to display "clear" only when needed to advance a train over the line. (As mentioned in the Chapter 1, some British lines used to leave signals displaying "clear" until the train passed, but this practice was altered after the accident at Abbots Ripton in 1875. In Britain after 1876, two-position lower-quadrant semaphores with solid red blades and flat ends would have been used as manual block signals. Practice has varied in other places, and since the development of more modern signal hardware, a great variety of signals has been used for manual block control.)

Before a train may enter a block, the operator controlling the entrance to that block must make sure that the

Recording train times at Enfield Cabin on the Dublin-Sligo line of Iarnród Éireann (Irish Rail). A train register is an important element of a manual block system. Here, a signalman records the times trains entered and exited the block. This adds an element of safety, so a train is not forgotten, and provides a written record of events in case of an abnormality.
Brian Solomon

block is clear. (An operator is a "signalman" in British practice, as used in Chapter 1. This text uses "operator" when describing predominantly American practice and "signalman" for predominantly British practice, because the positions, while similar, are not necessarily interchangable.) A rigid code of communication and operating rules establish a predetermined order of events to prepare a block in advance of a train.

Using an example based on British practice, consider two blocks, block AB and block BC, on a double-track line. A train needs to advance from A to C in the current of traffic. Signalman A, positioned at the entrance to block AB, asks his counterpart, Signalman B, if block AB is clear. If Signalman B responds that block AB is clear, Signalman A asks for permission to allow the train to advance through

block AB. If there is no reason to deny permission, signalman B will authorize it.

When this has been accomplished, Signalman A sets his signal to "clear," indicating to the locomotive driver ("engineer," in American terms) that block AB is clear of all trains, and the train may proceed. Once the train has entered AB, Signalman A then restores the signal to its most restrictive aspect—typically "stop"—to prevent following trains from entering the block.

Meanwhile, Signalman B, who also controls the signals for block BC, calls Signalman C and repeats the whole process. When the train exits AB and completely enters BC, Signalman B communicates with Signalman A to tell him the block is now clear.

In the strictest interpretation of the block system, if a train has not exited block AB or if other circumstances will prevent a train from safely traversing AB, when Signalman A initially contacts Signalman B to see if the block is clear, Signalman B will advise him that the block is not clear, and permission to enter the block cannot be granted. In this case, Signalman A will hold the signal at the entrance to AB in the stop position and force the oncoming train to stop and wait until the line is safe.

Operations on a single-track line are more complex, since blocks must be protected for both opposing and following moves. Since a head-on collision is one of the most destructive and thus most feared railway accidents, special precautions must be taken to prevent two trains from entering the same block from opposite directions. Before a train can be admitted to a block from either end, not only must the block be clear, the signalman must ensure that signals at the opposite end are displaying "stop" indications.

Each block station keeps a register—a written record—of the details relating to the clearing of signals and passage of trains through each block. A typical register would list the time each signalman came on duty, prevailing weather conditions, the times individual trains were given permission to enter each block, when the trains entered the block, and when they exited. Since each block has a block station at each end, there are two identical records for every block. The register provides a check for signalmen when clearing trains, adding a level of safety by reducing the chance for human error. It also provides a record in case of a problem or accident.

The signalman at Wicklow passes the staff to the driver of a passenger train as the train is moving. The driver will retain the staff until he gets to the end of the block at Rathdrum, where he will drop this staff and take the next one. Only when this staff is released and returned to the appropriate electric staff instrument may another staff be released. Brian Solomon

PERMISSIVE MANUAL BLOCK

Over time, manual block systems evolved to facilitate greater flexibility in operation, encompass more complex situations, and offer greater levels of safety. One simple way of increasing the flexibility of a block system that does not require significant new infrastructure is to use permissive blocking. In the basic example described above, absolute block is used. With absolute block, only one train is permitted in a block at any time. With permissive block, additional trains can follow a train through a block, typically with speed restrictions to ensure a level of protection to the first train.

Permissive block increases track capacity and allows for switching moves and other actions that may be hampered by the strictest interpretation of absolute block. Permissive operations were common in American practice. In a permissive manual block system, an operator (signalman) may display three aspects to trains. In addition to the basic "stop" and "proceed" aspects, a "permissive" or "caution" aspect may be displayed.

Permissive block used in conjunction with a timetable provides a level of protection for following moves. In most scenarios involving following movement, permissive manual block has been allowed for freight trains and other types of traffic that do not carry passengers. To provide maximum safety protection, passenger trains are typically excluded from permissive blocking.

Manual block has been easily adapted to accommodate the use of passing sidings, both in double-track territory, to allow a faster train to overtake a slower one, and in single-track territory, to facilitate the meeting and overtaking of trains. Where all trains operate in accordance with a timetable, the passing and meeting of trains can be predetermined through use of the schedule. A block system affords provisions for allowing trains in and out of sidings.

Often, passing sidings are conveniently located at block stations, making meeting and passing trains easier to facilitate and simpler to communicate.

ADVANCED MANUAL BLOCK SYSTEMS

Advanced telegraphic devices made safer and more flexible manual block systems possible. The development of block instruments with electric locks using relay circuits removed an element of human error from the manual block system. By using electric locks with mechanical interlocking, signals could not be set to "clear" at a block station unless operators at both ends of the section had set their instruments to "clear" for that block. This arrangement eliminates the potential for an operator/signalman to accidentally admit a

train into a block before the section is clear.

In Britain, the system of electrically interlocked block instruments is known as "Lock and Block" and became the predominant form of signaling on passenger lines in the late nineteenth century. Such systems were used to a more limited extent in both the United States and Canada. The addition of a track circuit in the manual block system provided another level of safety, because operators had positive knowledge of block occupancy.

The most basic manual block signaling arrangement presented undesirable capacity restraints. In addition to allowing only one train at a time in a block, trains needed to reduce their speed and be prepared to stop when approaching the home signal of block stations. With two-position signaling, a locomotive engineer had but two options at each block station: stop or proceed. Without any advance warning, an engineer had to assume the next signal would display "stop." To avoid the risk of overrunning a block signal (and colliding with a train stopped just beyond that

Staff system operation remains on the Bessemer & Lake Erie. Here at Albion, Pennsylvania, are the staff holders for Conneaut Branch (CX) and Erie Branch (FX) sections. Since this photo was taken in August 2000, the Erie branch has been converted to operation by Form X, a type of track warrant, after Norfolk Southern run-through trains began operating between Shenango and Wallace Junction. B&LE Rule 303 states, "The location of the staff will be specified in the Special Instructions. The staff must be returned to the specific location when the train or engine using it has finished with it and is clear of the designated track." Since there is only one staff for each section, only one train may operate at a time.
Patrick Yough

signal), the engineer had to operate at a reduced speed. However reducing speed, especially with a long, heavy train, would greatly slow a train's progress through each block and further limit capacity.

A simple way to speed up movements and give locomotive engineers greater warning of the position home signals is to provide a distant (or approach) signal to the home

A pair of "S-type" miniature electric staff instruments at Boyle cabin on Iarnród Éireann (Irish Rail). These simple machines are operated by the magneto generator seen to the left. Each instrument has a counterpart at the other end of the block. Only one staff at a time can be withdrawn from a connected pair of electric staff instruments, but each instrument holds extra staffs to accommodate an imbalance of traffic. Brian Solomon

signal. A distant signal mimics the condition of the home signal, except instead of displaying "stop" and "clear" ("proceed") aspects, it displays "approach" and "clear" aspects. A "stop" aspect is not needed at the distant signal if it is unnecessary to stop a train outside the block station. Therefore, all this signal must do is to slow the train if the block ahead is occupied. If a train receives a "clear" aspect at a distant signal, this indicates that it is safe to proceed at track speed, since the block signal will also display "clear."

In British practice, a distant signal is operated manually by the signalman at the beginning of the block. A distant signal cannot be cleared until the home signal is cleared first. In situations where greater warning is needed in block operation, an outer distant signal can be used. In situations where trains will routinely need to stop at a block station, a fixed distant signal may be used. A fixed distant signal is an immobile, one-aspect signal that displays only a cautionary aspect and simply warns a locomotive engineer that he is approaching a block station.

If the location of a block station coincides with a regular stopping point, such as a passenger station—which was standard in British practice—a starting signal at the far end of the station provides additional flexibility and safety. This can be useful for increasing capacity and keeping a railway both safe and fluid in situations on double-track where trains may be following each other in rapid succession. In this way, a train can proceed into a station and make its stop without having to wait for a train in the next block to clear that block. When the block ahead of the station is cleared, the train in the station can be given the signal to depart.

Variations of this arrangement are still used in Britain and Ireland but were not common in the United States and are not used in contemporary North American practice.

In many situations, block stations are combined with other facilities—passenger stations, passing sidings, junctions, and freight yards. The operators at block stations may also operate interlocking signals, so the block stations are located in an interlocking tower (known as a signal box in Britain). At quieter, simpler locations, the block station may be combined with a passenger or freight station or related facility, and the operator may be assigned other duties, such as selling tickets.

ADVANCED MANUAL BLOCK ON SINGLE-TRACK

Several varieties of advanced manual block systems have been devised for single-track, providing protection for opposing movements. The staff system requires the locomotive crew to have a physical staff in their possession to occupy a block. Possession of the staff is authorized by an operator/signalman at the entrance to the block and itself gives a train the authority to occupy the block. When a train reaches the end of the block, the staff is relinquished to the operator at that end, and a new staff is issued for the next block. Each block has its own distinctive staff, to avoid the staff from one block inadvertently being used on an adjacent block.

The limitations of the basic staff system are readily obvious. What if a train wishes to enter the block but the staff is at the far end? This type of control system is not well suited to operating successive trains in one direction and works efficiently only where traffic is evenly balanced in both directions. The solution to the inefficiencies of the staff system came with the development of more advanced telegraph technology.

The electric staff system uses interlocked machines at either end of the block. Each machine holds many staffs, but only one may be withdrawn at a time. Operators/signal-

men at both ends of the block must authorize the removal of a staff from either end. Once a staff is released, both machines lock electrically, and no further staffs may be removed until the first staff is replaced. Electric staff machines allow trains to follow one another safely over a line in succession or meet at block stations. Elaborate staff apparatus has been developed for more complex operations.

The signalman at Maynooth cabin in Ireland holds the staff used to authorize movements between Maynooth and Enfield on the Sligo Line. This staff is made of aluminum and is designed to fit in an "S-type" miniature electric staff instrument of the Webb-Thompson system, manufactured by the Railway Signal Company of London. To make sure that the correct staff has been issued, each one has the locations at each end of the block stamped into it. Brian Solomon

Although the electric staff system is no longer used in the United States, a number of lines once applied this system, among them Milwaukee Road, New Haven, Northern Pacific, Lackawanna, and Southern Pacific during the twentieth century. Electric staff systems remain in use in manual block territory in Britain and Ireland, among other countries.

While electric staff is no longer used in American practice, simple manual staff remains active on a few lines. Bessemer & Lake Erie uses this sytem to authorize movement on branch lines. This operation is covered by B&LE

The small interlocking frame at Rathdrum, Co. Wicklow, Ireland, controls switches and signals at the station. This station is located at one end of a manual block that extends from Wicklow (town) to Rathdrum and at the other end from here to Arklow. Notice the electric staff instrument in the left-hand corner of the cabin. Brian Solomon

Rules 301 to 306. For example, Rule 302 states, "No train or engine may enter territory where Rule 301 is in effect without having possession of the designated staff unless protected in both directions by Rule 99. A train or engine having possession of the staff may move in either direction on the designated track without flag protection."

B&LE Rule 306 states, "Trains must not take possention of a staff without permission from the Train Movement Director."

CONTROLLED MANUAL BLOCK

In America, a system called Controlled Manual Block was used to ensure a greater level of protection in manual block territory. This system used electrically interlocked signaling machines and track circuit that required the cooperation of operators at both ends of the block to set the direction of traffic over the line and to clear blocks. The level of protection for following and opposing moves this system offered was sufficient to permit trains to move strictly by signal indication. If prescribed by railroad rules, operation on Controlled Manual Block allowed for the signals to supersede timetable authority, and operation by signal indication replaced the need for written authority given by train orders.

Controlled Manual Block installations would often be coordinated with interlocking plants. On single-track lines, meets were made at passing sidings. Sometimes these sidings were located at block stations, but they could also be located remotely. Also, as train lengths grew, sidings were extended, and the far end of a siding might be a considerable distance from a block station. In Britain, switches on running tracks were controlled by signalmen, but in the United States, hand-throw switches for passing sidings remain quite common. In these situations the train crew,

rather than an operator, is responsible for lining switches.

To allow for adequate signal protection and reasonable operational flexibility, complex electrical circuits, using numerous relays and track circuits, were developed for Controlled Manual Block operation. These allowed trains to enter passing sidings at remote locations, to permit safe meets on single-track. Operations using Controlled Manual Block were greatly aided by the use of trackside telephones, which permitted train crews to contact signalmen at block stations for instructions regarding meets and other complicated moves, such as online switching, or the addition and removal of helpers in graded territory.

COMMUNICATION CODES

In traditional railroading, the only effective way of communicating with trains was through the use of signals. Once a train passed a block station and the signals it controlled, it was effectively out of communication, so it was imperative to impart any instructions regarding a train's movement at block stations.

Signalmen in block stations communicated block information with one another using either telegraph or railroad telephone. Traditionally, this communication was made with numeric signal codes, which had fixed meanings, to ensure that the message conveyed was entirely clear. Typically, the codes were transmitted by telegraph. In British practice, these were telegraphic bell codes that sounded audible bells in the signal box. In America, a telegraph key or telephone was employed.

The codes were strictly defined in the railway rulebook, with which all employees involved in operations were required to be familiar. The rules contained provisions for

Radio-controlled track switches can be used on lines in dark territory. This radio-controlled switch located on the Bessemer & Lake Erie at Conneaut, Ohio, is operated from the locomotive cab. Track authority is provided under Bessemer's Rules 301 to 306, covering movements by the staff system. Patrick Yough

communications failures and allowed for limited movement of trains in situations where the normal procedures could not be followed. Safety always takes precedence over efficiency. Many railways had different procedures for the operation of freight and passenger trains through manual blocks, with passenger train rules being more restrictive, to

provide a greater level of safety. For this reason, passenger train codes were distinctive from those of freight trains.

In Britain, more elaborate codes were developed, enabling signalmen to describe the different types of rail traffic. This was in part due to different braking requirements, as a result of different braking systems in use, and varying speeds at which different classes of trains traveled.

In the earliest manual block arrangements, each railway had its own distinctive code that best suited its operations. Over time, standardized codes were implemented. Despite regional and even national standardization, telegraphic codes were different in the United States and Great Britain. In Britain and Ireland, bell codes remain in use today.

Here is an example of the manual block communicating code as recommended by the signal section of the Association of American Railroads in Chapter XXII of their 1937 publication, *American Railway Signaling Principle and Practices*:

Rule 316 codes,

1	Display Stop-signal.
13	I understand.
17	Display Stop-signal. Train following.
2	Block Clear.
3	Block wanted for train other than passenger.
36	Block wanted for passenger train.
4	Train other than passenger has entered block.
46	Passenger train has entered block.
5	Block is not clear of train other than passenger.
56	Block is not clear of passenger train.
7	Train following.
8	Opening block station. Answer by 2, 5, or 56.
9	Closing block station (to be followed by a 2).

The numbers represent code sent over telegraph or telephone. As late as the 1950s, various types of manual block signaling accounted for control of roughly 28,000 miles of line in the United States. Today, traditional manual block is relatively unusual. These systems have been replaced by more modern signal systems, including automatic block and Centralized Traffic Control.

TOWERS AND INTERLOCKING

INTERLOCKING MECHANISMS are used at junctions, crossings, and other places where railway routes are joined. The primary purpose of an interlocking is to ensure that no train is authorized to enter the interlocked junction, crossing, or movable bridge unless the route through the track layout (sometimes referred to as the "interlocking plant") is safe for occupancy. Briefly, safety checks ensure that the route is complete (all switches lined and locked for movement on the desired route) and that no other conflicting or opposing movement is authorized that would endanger a train's safety. An interlocking can use mechanical or electrical controls or a combination of the two to ensure that signals and switches are in proper positions. An increasing number of interlockings use microprocessor-based logic to perform safety assurance.

The interlocking signal tower is a traditional symbol of railroading. Although the manned tower is now considered obsolete, a few remain. An eastbound CSX coal train passes the closed former Baltimore & Ohio tower at Mountain Lake Park, Maryland, on October 15, 1994. Brian Solomon operation allow for the centralization of control through the use of automatic and remote operation of both switches and signals. Interlocking operators typically have the benefit of a schematic diagram that depicts the relative location of switches and signals and provides numbers that correspond with control levers. With the use of track circuitry, indication lights can be incorporated on the diagram that show the position of trains in relation to the interlocking plant. In addition, track circuits combined with enunciator bells give operators audible warning of approaching trains.

Traditionally, interlocking plants were controlled from an elevated tower. Today, interlockings are often controlled remotely from dispatchers' consoles, which can be located hundreds or thousands of miles from the switch plant. In America, interlocking towers are typically under the authority of the train dispatcher, and a tower operator would be in communication with the dispatcher for instructions. Often, a dispatcher issues the operator instructions only if an unusual scenario arises and leaves him alone under normal circumstances.

A tower operator typically lines trains through the plant based on their normal pattern. An employees' timetable or a list of scheduled moves may be the operator's general routing guide. Sometimes, tower operators need to communicate with one another to coordinate moves and alert each other to impending traffic. Traditionally, some interlocking towers may have controlled sections of manual block beyond the immediate interlocking, thereby serving as block stations as well as interlocking towers.

Signalman Donal Flynn works the mechanical levers at Iarnród Éireann's (Irish Rail's) Killucan cabin on the Dublin-Sligo line on May 3, 2002. This traditional mechanical interlocking was one of 50 still in daily service in Ireland as of 2001. Killucan, like most Irish Rail cabins, uses a lever frame made by the Railway Signal Company. The levers are color coded: red for stop (home) signals, green for distant signals, black for switch points, blue for locking bars, and white to indicate a spare (unused) lever. Brian Solomon

MECHANICAL INTERLOCKING

This signal pipeline compensator accommodates natural temperature-related expansion and contraction. Even slight changes in length can affect the performance of the pipes and wires that operate switch and signal mechanisms.
Brian Solomon

Various interlocking controls have been applied to railroad applications. The oldest type is the all-mechanical system, using direct mechanical linkage from levers to control switches, signals, and other track elements, such as derails. A system of pipelines (or, in some countries, rods and wires) transmits power from the control levers to equipment in the field. These levers are moved manually, and the working of a mechanical plant requires able-bodied operators who have the strength to move points and signals, which can be located a considerable distance from the tower.

A mechanical interlocking uses a grid of metal bars with notches and protrusions that present mechanical interference unless the levers are operated in a predetermined sequence. In this way, the machine physically prevents a signal operator from lining a conflicting route or setting a signal for a route that has not been lined. Because of its dependence on physical force, mechanical interlocking has inherent limitations in terms of the distance of the switches and signals operated via pipeline.

One potential cause of accidents is the movement of switches beneath moving trains. To prevent this from happening, switches have both a lock lever and a lever that moves the points. To set a switch, it must be unlocked, lined, and locked into place. Only when this is done and there are no other conflicts can a signal be cleared for a train to use that switch.

Usually a route needs to be lined up through an interlocking plant. This may involve only one switch or crossing, or it may involve a whole network of switches and crossings. If a route has been lined and locked, another route that conflicts with it cannot be lined until the first route has been restored. One interesting facet of any interlocking plant is that a properly trained operator working a properly functioning machine should never encounter resistance from the machine. The machine is there to provide added safety by augmenting railroad rules and the operator's judgment.

Baltimore & Ohio's "Z" Tower at Keyser, West Virginia, is an electro-mechanical plant that opened in 1906. As of this writing in 2003, it is still in service. Seen here on October 18, 2002, "Z" still serves an important role in CSX operations on the old B&O West End. Now known as the Mountain Subdivision, it is one of the most difficult graded mainlines in the Eastern United States. In the foreground are the pipeline rods used to operate switches and switch locks. Brian Solomon

ELECTRO-MECHANICAL

An electromechanical plant combines elements of a mechanical interlocking with electric controls. In a typical scenario, switches are controlled through mechanical linkages, while signals are controlled electrically. Such a plant still relies on a mechanical interlocking mechanism to prevent conflicts. An electromechanical plant may control some switches electrically.

One advantage of this type of plant is that it allows easier control of signals further from the plant, overcoming one drawback of all-mechanical plants. Another advantage (and indeed the most common use) is the ability to add functions to an existing frame without physically extending the machine. This often coincided with the replacement of mechanical semaphores with power signals that were operated from the electric frame bolted to the top of (and interlocked with) the original mechanical frame.

ELECTRIC INTERLOCKING

This type of machine uses a mechanical interlocking frame but powers both signals and switches electrically. An electric plant does not face the limitations imposed by the

A detailed view of the pipeline rods and rollers at "Z" tower. The pipeline connect the large mechanical levers with the switch locks and switch points. It can take a lot of strength to move a set of remote switch points on a cold day at a mechanical plant. Brian Solomon

strength of an operator and allows for the control of signals and switches at greater distances from the interlocking machine than is possible with mechanical linkages. An electric plant can be used to reduce the number of levers required, because some functions, such as locking, can be combined with electric controls. The operation of a crossover, or slip switch, which would require several levers in a mechanical plant, needs just one lever in an electric plant. Also, an electric plant is wired so that when a route is locked, the power to switch machines is cut, to prevent the accidental realignment of points beneath the wheels of a train.

⮕ This February 21, 2003, view of outbound Metra suburban passenger trains at A2 Tower in Chicago, shows three types of signal hardware on the signal bridges. Chicago & North Western, which operated the tracks on the left, used searchlight signals, and GRS used horizontally oriented color-light signals. Milwaukee Road used trackage rights over the PRR Panhandle that featured PRR's standard position-light signals. Brian Solomon

⮕ Metra's A2 tower, northwest of Chicago's Union Station, controls a busy junction between passenger lines out of both Union Station and North Western Terminal. Although a Milwaukee Road tower, it was built in 1938 to Pennsylvania Railroad specifications, because Milwaukee used PRR's Panhandle route to reach Union Station. Originally, this machine featured an 83-lever interlocking. Today, fewer levers are in service. It is a surviving example of a Union Switch & Signal Model-14 electropneumatic interlocking. A horizontal mechanical interlocking bed prevents the lining of conflicting moves. According to *Railway Signaling*, at the time of installation, an all-relay machine was considered but was deemed impractical and too costly. Brian Solomon

ELECTROPNEUMATIC

Very similar to an electric interlocking, an electropneumatic plant uses air-actuated switch machines powered by air lines from a central pneumatic station. Pneumatic interlocking permits switch points to move more quickly, making this type of plant popular at large terminals, where trains operated at close headways over complex track arrangements. Although popular on some lines in the early twentieth century, pneumatic signals using a specialized semaphore design were out of favor for new installations by the 1920s.

Baltimore & Ohio's Altamont Tower is located atop the famous 17-Mile Grade on CSX's Mountain Subdivision in western Maryland. In steam days, a wye was located here to turn helpers. A GRS all-relay interlocking plant was installed at Altamont about 1952, to replace an earlier electro-mechanical plant. Pictured here is the operator's desk with a GRS control machine, used to set switches and signals. Above the machine, to the left of the black phone, is the time lock. Altamont closed in the mid-1990s, but the building remains. Brian Solomon

Baltimore & Ohio's "ND" Tower at Viaduct Junction in Cumberland, Maryland, on October 16, 1994. By the 1990s, this tower blended technology spanning more than one hundred years. The traditional lever frame was that of the Saxby & Farmer patent. Switches and signals were not mechanically locked and instead used all-relay interlocking. The track diagram panel with signal levers is visible to the left, beyond the mechanical levers. The tower controlled an important junction on the west side of Cumberland, between the Mountain and Main Line Subdivisions. Brian Solomon

INTERLOCKING ALL-RELAY AND ELECTRONIC

This type of plant uses electronic circuitry in place of mechanical components for interlocking protection. An all-relay plant further reduces the size of control levers, allowing pushbutton control. Electronic circuits allow more advanced control, such as GRS's NX (eNtrance-eXit; see Chapter 2) routing. This system allows the operator to select a route through a plant by choosing the entrance and exit points, which greatly simplifies the amount of work required on the part of the operator.

In addition to automatic routing, many electronic interlocking systems work in conjunction with track circuitry, allowing operators to set signals to function as automatic block signals once a route has been lined. This is a useful feature if trains are following one another in succession over a common route. Advances such as automatic routing are part of a trend in American railroading to replace labor with technology. All-relay control, automatic route selection, and electrically controlled switches and signals give a tower operator the ability to control far more territory than was possible with earlier interlocking systems.

From the 1920s onward, railways were able to consolidate towers by installing all-relay plants. With all-relay plants, a location that may have had two or more mechanical interlockings and several operators could easily be run by just one skilled operator from a central location. All-relay interlocking, combined with Centralized Traffic Control (see Chapter 5), led to the blending of interlocking and block signal systems. With the miniaturization of electronic components, electromechanical relay circuits have given way to solid-state equipment. Today, an interlocking can be controlled from a computer console with a mouse.

The operator's board and lighted diagram at Chicago Metra's A5 tower. This was built as an all-relay electric interlocking. The top row of levers operates switches that are set for either "normal" or "reverse." The bottom row of levers controls signals. The buttons at the bottom can be used to set "call on" signals that can display a "restricting" aspect immediately after a train has passed. This is done to expedite moves over the same route through the plant. Tower A5 now also governs movements through other nearby interlockings, using computer controls. Brian Solomon

The former Milwaukee Road A5 tower (Pacific Junction) is a busy location on Chicago's Metra. This tower was built during 1941 and 1942 and was commissioned on August 15, 1942. It used an all-relay electric interlocking machine to replace an earlier mechanical plant with 104 working levers. When it opened, there were approximately 200 moves a day through the plant. Since that time, a few tracks have been lifted and the diamond crossing has been removed. Brian Solomon

➲ Many railroads use three-head signals at interlockings. This tall mast and bracket signal were located on New York Central's Big Four route at Morgan Tower. The top blades were for normal-speed route aspects, and the bottom blades could be used for slow-speed and/or restricting aspects. On this particular signal, the middle arms are fixed in the red position, because medium-speed aspects were unnecessary here. Notice that only the red roundels are in place on the middle arms. C. E. Helms; Jay Williams collection

🎧 Interlocking signals can display a variety of aspects to govern the moves of trains through complex junctions. Some railroads, such as the Baltimore & Ohio, used speed aspects that indicated how fast a train could travel, while other lines used route signals. The left-hand Baltimore & Ohio color-position-light displays "stop." The right-hand signal displays "approach slow"—two green lights one above the other with a yellow marker. The aspect is determined by the color and position of the lights, and by the position of the marker. This signal at Curtis, Indiana, is unusual, because it featured marker lights for all six positions. Brian Solomon

ROUTE LOCKING

Interlocking is necessary to provide a safety check in case the person operating signal controls makes an error. One potential problem that can occur with an interlocking arrangement is if an operator, after lining and locking a route and setting up signals, decides to change the route as a train is approaching. A train could accept a signal through the plant, only to find that the route is no longer lined. If a conflicting route has been set up, an accident could result.

To prevent this from happening, interlocking controls are equipped with route locking, using time locks to keep an operator from changing signals and switches directly in front of an oncoming train or when a train is occupying the plant. Once a route has been set up, it cannot immediately be altered or canceled. Timelocks must be actuated to release the route only after a specified time has elapsed.

During this time, all signals on the route and any that may conflict are locked in their most restrictive positions. The locking time depends on several considerations, including the type of traffic through the interlocking and the weight and speed of trains, which can affect braking distances. Time locking can be as short as 30 seconds and as long as several minutes. To an operator who accidentally sets up an incorrect route, the relatively short interval imposed by the time lock may seem like an eternity—at a busy plant every second counts, and delaying a train unnecessarily can result in a management inquiry.

In normal operation, if the route is not canceled and a train passes through the plant, time locking is not actuated when altering the route for following moves.

"Approach locking" provides an operator with greater flexibility. Under this system, an operator can cancel a route after it has been set up provided nothing is occupying the circuit on the route and nothing is "on approach" to the route. This last part is crucial. When a train is on approach to the route, the route is locked and must go into time if the operator wishes to cancel it. The route will be unlocked when a train passes through it. With approach locking, the

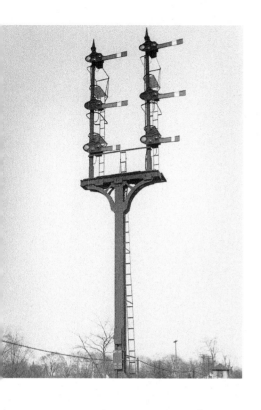

Illinois Central did not assign specific speeds to most of its signal indications. The near color-light signal seen here on IC's Chicago-Champaign main line at Gilman, Illinois (looking south) displays a yellow over green over red aspect, designated on IC as Rule 808 "approach diverging." The following signal is red over green, Rule 809, "diverging clear." The red signal in the distance is not part of the same route as the other two; this is an automatic block signal (with number plate) mounted on the same mast as the northward absolute signal for Gilman. Since braking distance between the two near signals in the picture is insufficient, the signal that precedes them (about a mile and a half behind the photographer) displays an "Approach" for such a diverging move at Gilman. Pete Ruesch

operator is not committed to a route until a train is on approach to it. Thus, if he needed to change the route and no trains were on approach, he could do so quickly, without a penalty from time locking.

Further flexibility is offered with sequential release, which releases portions of the route as they are cleared by the train. In a long or complicated interlocking, sequential release can speed an operator's ability to line trains through.

INTERLOCKING SIGNALS

At interlockings, different sets of rules apply to the operation of trains than on the line. Since switches and signals are under the direct control of a skilled operator, train movements are governed by signal indications within interlocking limits.

Because the rules at interlockings are different from operations in block signal territory, interlocking signals must be distinguished from other types of line-side signals. Interlocking signals are normally absolute signals, meaning that a stop aspect must be obeyed as "stop and stay." Railroads have used a variety of techniques to distinguish interlocking signals. Some lines use three-head signals

at interlockings; others use line-side signs to post interlocking limits. In addition, interlocking signals are typically distinguished by their lack of a numberplate.

SPEED SIGNALS VERSUS ROUTE SIGNALS

A fixed signal at an interlocking may be used to control a variety of routes. Initially, interlocking signals were "route signals," which indicated that a main route or diverging route was lined up. After about 1900, "speed signaling" gained popularity in the United States, particularly on large eastern lines, such as the Pennsylvania, New York Central, and Baltimore and Ohio Railroads. Speed signals indicate the speed of the route taken rather than a specific diverging route.

With interlocking speed signals, the indications govern the speed through interlocking limits, which are typically based on the speed of switches. Speed signaling rules have also been applied to block signals, as described in Chapter 5. The basic speeds are normal speed (the normal maximum mainline speed); limited speed, often defined as 45 mph;

SPEED SIGNALS EXAMPLE

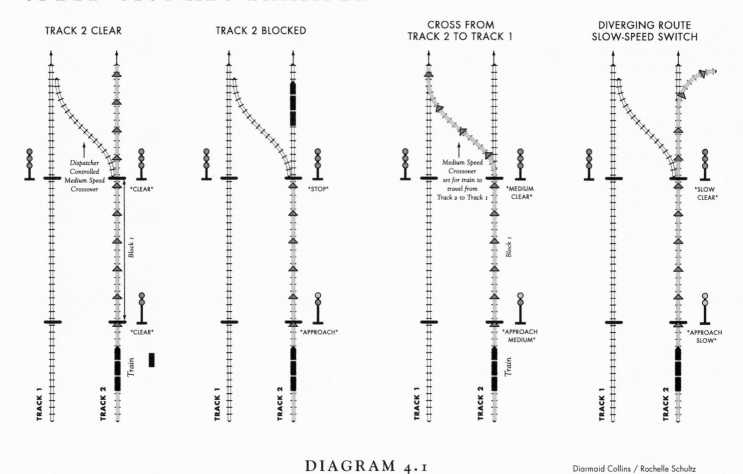

TRACK 2 CLEAR   TRACK 2 BLOCKED   CROSS FROM TRACK 2 TO TRACK 1   DIVERGING ROUTE SLOW-SPEED SWITCH

DIAGRAM 4.1   Diarmaid Collins / Rochelle Schultz

medium speed, often 30 mph; slow speed, which is 15 to 20 mph; and restricted speed, which has special implications for interlocking signals. "Restricted" is usually used to indicate that a track may be occupied, so trains should travel at 15 mph or less and expect to stop short of trains or obstructions (see the glossary). It can be used to allow another train to pass a stop signal after a train has passed or to occupy a track not equipped with track circuits.

Speed signals have been used to convey a variety of information a locomotive engineer needs to safely negotiate an interlocking with minimal delay. With simple train operations, such detailed information may seem unnecessary, but when train weights and lengths vary, speed signals can be useful in expediting train movements through complex trackage.

For example, the Baltimore & Ohio operated a variety of traffic over the same tracks. In some places, express long-distance trains, short commuter trains, fast freight, and long, heavy coal trains would all use the same tracks

and negotiate the same interlockings. The maximum travel speed and braking characteristics of these trains can vary considerably. Speed signaling will help an engineer anticipate what may happen next.

In the days before radio communication, a dispatcher or operator who needed to communicate with moving trains used signal indications. The use of track circuits in combination with interlocking signals, allowing trains to follow each other through interlocking routes, contributed the need for complex speed indications.

The four examples in Diagram 4.1 show the aspects of a distant signal and a home signal at a simple interlocking on a double-track mainline. The rules cited are similar to the rules now applied by the Northeast Operating Rules Advisory Committee (NORAC).

In the first example, a train has a clear track and thus receives "clear" aspects at both distant and home signals. In the second example, a second train is one full block ahead, causing the distant signal to display "approach" and the

88

home signal to display "stop" in the same pattern of normal automatic block signals. In the third example, the route ahead is clear but the train is lined to cross from mainline track 2 to mainline track 1, so it receives an "approach medium" from the distant signal and "medium clear" from the home signal. "Medium clear" is defined by standard Rule 283 as "medium speed through switches, crossovers, sidings, and over power operated switches; then proceed [at normal speed]." In the rule, "at normal speed" is implied.

In the fourth example, the route ahead is clear, but the train is lined for a slow speed diverging route (not shown in the early examples for the sake of simplicity). In this last case, the distant signal displays "approach slow," which Rule 284 defines as "proceed approaching the next signal at slow speed. Trains exceeding medium speed must begin reduction to that speed as soon as the engine passes the 'approach slow' signal [aspect]."

Since "approach slow" is a medium speed signal, the train can continue at medium speed until it approaches the next signal. The difference between medium speed and slow speed is 15 mph, which can be significant, depending on the length of a block. The next signal is "slow clear," which Rule 287 defines as "proceed at slow speed until entire train clears all interlocking or spring switches, then proceed at

normal speed." Notice that "slow clear" applies only to the interlocking limits and does not regulate train speed once the train is fully on the diverging route. In general, speed signaling is not used to govern normal track speed.

If route signaling were used instead of speed signaling, as in the third and fourth examples, the distant signal might show "approach diverging," which can be defined as "proceed prepared to advance on diverging route at the next signal at prescribed speed through switches." The home signal would then display "diverging clear," which can indicate "proceed on diverging route at prescribed speed through switches." The rule for various diverging routes is the same regardless of the aspect displayed.

Route signaling may still provide aspects that indicate if a left diverging route or a right diverging route is to be taken, but since the signals do not govern speed, the locomotive engineer must rely on knowledge of the line to know how fast a train can safely negotiate switches.

↻ On the former Boston & Albany mainline, at Framingham, Massachusetts, a Massachusetts Bay Transportation Authority commuter train gets a "medium clear" aspect to cross from the No. 2 main track to the No. 1. This aspect is displayed by red over green over red. Brian Solomon

When Boston's South Station opened in 1898–99, it was the busiest terminal in the world. In June 1963, a pair of New Haven Railroad FL9s leads a New York–bound train under signal bridge No. 7. These signals were controlled from Tower 1, seen to the left of the train. Beyond the tower is signal bridge No. 6. Notice that each set of signals has a letter plate below it. These are all two-position lower-quadrant semaphores; this train has an "approach" aspect on outbound signal "V." Signals "Q" and "U" were not used at the time of the photo, so their blades and letter plates had been removed.

Jim Shaughnessy

ROUTES THROUGH COMPLEX INTERLOCKINGS

A route that lines a train through a medium speed switch followed by a slow speed switch has special considerations, especially when several trains of differing weights are following one another. Here, the "medium approach slow" aspect can be used. Rule 283-B defines this as "Medium speed through switches, crossovers, sidings, and over power operated switches; then proceed, approaching next signal at slow speed."

This rule instructs a train to move at 30 mph through the first set of switches and then to expect a slow speed aspect at the next signal, for which it will need to reduce speed to 15 mph without being required to stop at that signal. The next signal will not display an aspect more restricting than "slow approach," which Rule 288 defines as "slow speed through switches, crossovers, sidings, and over power operated switches; then proceed, prepared to stop at next signal." A simpler solution would be to keep all trains moving slowly, but at a busy junction this can cause bottlenecks, and railroads often need to get traffic through an interlocking as quickly as is safe.

TOWERS

Interlocking towers were one of the traditional symbols of railroading. At one time thousands of towers were in use all across the United States. Here switchmen, operators, train directors, and train dispatchers regulated the flow of traffic through crucial points on the railroad. From the tower, employees could keep a close eye on operations. When routes were set, switches lined and locked, and signals cleared, the roar of a locomotive and the clatter of wheels soon followed. Trains would often pass within a few feet of the tower, so the men and women working there could see the faces of their fellows in the cabs of the trains they directed. Railroading was personal in those days, and the faces were often friends or close acquaintances.

Tower operators learned railroading on the ground. They spent months in training, learning the ins and outs of interlocking operation. They would spend weeks qualifying on their first tower, to comprehend the normal order of events. A good tower operator needed to anticipate events, to ensure that the railroad ran smoothly and efficiently. By thinking ahead and planning moves accordingly, trains could pass with minimal delay and maximum safety. A mistake on the operator's part would normally result only in delays, because the interlocking mechanisms should prevent collisions and other mishaps.

A busy tower may have seemed like an operating maelstrom to the novice. Trains would pass at short intervals, each often needing different routing or special attention. Annunciator bells rang, lights flashed, phones rang, dispatchers and timetables needed consultation, and the constant need to work levers made for hectic, busy work. One mistake and the signals would go into time, tying up the plant. Trains might be delayed, and the dispatcher

would be annoyed, or worse. When a technical problem arose, a maintainer had to be summoned, and quickly.

By contrast, a quiet tower might have seen only a few trains a day and have been a relatively sleepy place, yet after hours of inaction and waiting, the operator would need to spring into action and move a number of levers in quick succession—making for a case of "wait and hurry up."

Once a tower operator mastered one interlocking, he could then more easily qualify on others. It was typical for junior employees to work "relief" jobs, covering the days

The "tower" at Brewster, New York, on New York Central's Harlem Division was located inside the station. Featuring a small machine worked by the agent-operator, it controlled switches and signals north (railroad direction west) of the station. These led in three directions: to the single main track to Chatham; into Put Junction Yard, where most of the passenger trains originated or terminated; and to the wye, which at the time of this photo on March 15, 1958, still connected to the Putnam Division. *Richard Jay Solomon*

more senior operators were off. By working "relief," an operator might regularly work in two or more towers to earn a full week's pay. By qualifying in more places, the operator would have more opportunities to work. This practice encouraged tower operators to gain familiarity with a whole line or region. Eventually, a junior employee might find a

regular tower to work in. Railroads traditionally promoted operators to dispatchers, which ensured that a dispatcher had a clear understanding of how the railroad worked. Dispatchers gave instructions to operators, and both jobs were easier when the person giving instructions could clearly visualize what needed to be done.

The day of the manned trackside interlocking tower is rapidly coming to a close in the United States. For more than a hundred years, there has been a deliberate, gradual trend toward greater centralization of control. In the days of strictly mechanical interlocking, the lengths of rods and wires limited the size of a plant a single tower could control. Technological advances such as those described earlier have made ever wider and more expansive control possible. The introduction of CTC and solid-state electronics has facilitated an age of remote-control railroading. This has allowed the closure and remote operation of even the most complex towers.

Some day, the last traditional tower in the United States may close, and an era will have passed. As a result of different cost-accounting or operating philosophies, other

Sunset on the tower at Tuscola, Illinois. Steve Smedley

countries have been less hasty to implement complete centralization of train control. There, more towers remain.

Tower rationalization is implemented primarily to save money. Computer-aided dispatching may be as safe as localized control, but is it as efficient? While railroads gain cost efficiency, they lose an element of operational efficiency. The railroad itself has become just an abstract schematic diagram to those controlling train movements. There are few operators to promote to train dispatchers, so train dispatchers must learn their trade in other ways. Dispatching offices are far from the tracks they control. Instead of a train rolling past the tower window with a person behind

In the steam era, thousands of interlocking towers were used in the United States, many controlling small junctions and crossings. The Malinta, Ohio, tower protected the crossing of the Detroit, Toledo & Ironton and Nickel Plate Road's Cloverleaf District and served as a train order station. This view, looking east on the Nickel Plate Road, was made on June 1, 1947. The two sets of semaphores near the tower are train order signals. C. E. Helms; Jay Williams collection

Interior view of Union Pacific's Ridgley Tower on the former Alton Route at Springfield, Illinois. Steve Smedley

the throttle, a train is little more than a colored line with a symbol and route indication on a video monitor. The people running that train are only distant voices on a radio.

Most interlockings are now little more than intersections of steel protected by silent sentinels and controlled by people and machines who can neither see nor hear the workings of the plant. Subtle indicators of potential problems once readily perceived by operators on the scene, such as snow or ice, poor visibility, possible vandalism, or accidents waiting to happen, cannot easily enter into an operator's judgment half a continent away.

Bonds at rail joints are necessary to maintain track circuit continuity. This view was made along the old Southern Pacific in the Oregon Cascades at Fuego on July 18, 2002. The line is now operated by Union Pacific. Note the cantilever signal bridge used to hold signals over two tracks. Tom Kline

TRACK CIRCUITS

The track circuit is a fundamental component for most North American signaling systems. It is key to the operation of automatic block signals (ABS), Centralized Traffic Control (CTC), cab signals, and many forms of automatic train control, as well as grade-crossing signals. The track circuit has also been applied to interlocking networks and manual block systems, to provide a greater level of safety and increased line capacity.

For the track circuit to work, a railway line must be divided into sections electrically isolated from each other by insulated rail joints. The basic system developed by Robinson (see Chapter 1) used for simple automatic block indications involves two circuits and a relay. Current is applied to the tracks so that each rail is part of the circuit, along with a track relay. Current flows from an electrical source, typically a low-voltage battery, along the line through one rail, then through a resistor and track relay,

A Southern Pacific westbound freight passes two sets of US&S Style-B lower-quadrant semaphores on the Tucumcari Line in January 1994. SP took control of this route from the El Paso & Southwestern in the 1920s and replaced Hall Style-K upper-quadrant semaphores with the older-style lower-quadrant signals, to maintain consistency. Brian Solomon

returning through the other rail to complete the circuit.

When the track is clear, the current passing through the rails energizes the track relay so that its armature rises, completing a secondary circuit that displays a "clear" aspect. This secondary circuit is electrically isolated from the track circuit, so the relay acts as a simple on/off switch.

When the wheels of a train enter the circuit, the all-metal wheel-axle pair acts as an electrical conductor and bridges the gap between the rails, providing a path of lower resistance than the one offered by the track relay. This "shunts" the track circuit, causing the relay to de-energize, dropping the armature and breaking the circuit for the clear

signal while simultaneously connecting a secondary circuit that displays a "stop" aspect.

Following failsafe principles, the relay must be energized to display a clear signal. Any loss of power in the track circuit caused by a failing battery, broken rail, or other disruption, will de-energize the relay and establish a circuit to display a "stop" aspect. An extremely important element of any signal system is to prevent signals from falsely displaying "clear" or less restrictive signals when more restrictive aspects should be displayed. This most fundamental track circuit is basically a building block for the more complex signal circuitry found in actual practice.

A track circuit has a variety of special circumstances that differentiate it from a normal electric circuit, such those used by commercial power grids in homes or in common electrical appliances. Common electric circuits use highly conductive wires to transmit current and highly resistant materials to insulate wires, to prevent stray

Chicago & North Western semaphores at Hammond, Wisconsin, at sunset on October 23, 1989, about a year before they were replaced. John Leopard

currents and undesired current flow. This is not the case with track circuits, where current must flow through iron or steel rails, which have lower conductivity than copper wire and do not have the high degree of insulation of normal wires.

By the nature of the primary service they provide the rails are open to the elements. The resistance between the rails can be much lower than between insulated wires and varies considerably with changes in prevailing weather conditions. Resistance is provided by the track structure—the cross ties and ballast. This resistance is higher when the trackbed is dry but lower when it is wet. The higher conductivity of waterlogged ballast and ties reduces the natural resistance of the track structure, so a track circuit must be designed to accommodate changes in the resistance between the rails caused by rain or snow.

Further complicating the situation are trace chemicals dropped from passing trains that can also lower the resistance. Iron and steel particles shaved off the rails, salt, and other chemicals can make for a reasonably conductive "soup" when ballast becomes saturated with water. If ballast and the track sub-bed function properly, water will drain away quickly and wash undesirable chemicals from the rails. However, conditions may develop whereby the electrolytic chemicals in the ballast perform as a simple battery, generating stray currents that can interfere with the basic track circuit.

Steel rails present low conductivity, limiting the practical length of a track circuit. A conventional direct-current circuit may cover just a mile or so of track. To improve the conductivity of the rails, electrical bonds bridge rail joints where a loss in conductivity may occur. To function properly in most circumstances, a track circuit must be designed with careful consideration for the sum of conductances needed to maintain the circuit through the rails. Since resistance increases as temperature increases, a track relay must have sufficient conductance to maintain the circuit and not drop because of changes in temperature or weather conditions. Yet it must still offer greater resistance than the wheels of a passing train, so the relay has no chance of remaining energized when it should drop.

Debris on the rails, rust, grease, and sand all present operating hazards. It is a serious situation when a train occupies a functioning track circuit but fails to shunt the circuit because of insulating material on the rails. In this situation, a signal would continue to display "clear," even though a train occupies the circuit. Normally, the great weight of a locomotive and cars, combined with the force of steel wheels rolling over steel rails, will break through any accumulated insulating material on the tracks.

In some circumstances, railways have found it necessary to prevent or restrict the operation of lightweight vehicles without additional protection, since such vehicles may not shunt track circuits reliably. For example, many American railroads now use lightweight track-based maintenance equipment, such as ballast regulators, tampers, and hyrail vehicles (conventional over-the-road trucks fitted with railway wheels for operation on tracks). Since this equipment may not necessarily shunt track circuits on a mainline, it requires absolute authority from a train dispatcher for operation.

In addition, railroad rules often have provisions for light locomotives (running singly without cars) and short or lightweight trains that may not shunt track circuits. For example, the Northeast Operating Rules Advisory Committee (NORAC), which recommends operating rules for dozens of railways in the Northeastern United States, including Amtrak, CSX, and Norfolk Southern, states in Rule 506,

> *Trains that might not shunt track circuits must not be operated in ABS territory without authority of the Dispatcher. Following movements must not be permitted between TBS's [temporary block stations], interlockings or controlled points directed by Form D line 13 to operate at Restricted Speed. Blocking devices must be applied to protect against following movements. The signal governing entrance to the affected track may be displayed to authorize train movements, but must be immediately restored to Stop position once the non-shunting train has entered the block.*

> *The Dispatcher or Operator admitting the train to the block must notify the Dispatcher or Operator in charge of adjoining territory that the train is of a type that might not shunt track circuits. Where Rule 261 [track signaled for movements in both directions, where signal indication authorizes train movements] is in effect, this notification must be given prior to admitting the train to the block, and the Dispatcher or Operator in charge of adjoining territory must provide blocking device protection against opposing movements.*

Fundamentally, since the automatic block cannot be relied upon to protect lightweight equipment, this rule reverts to the protection provided by the principles of the manual block system.

In some countries, such as Ireland, the use of sand to increase adhesion was banned, for fear it would interfere with track circuitry. This is not generally true in the United

States, where locomotives automatically apply sand to the rail when slippage is detected. However, some restrictions govern the application of sand and the use of certain types of equipment on sanded rail. For example, the *General Code of Operating Rules*, Rule 9.22, states, "Do not allow an engine with less than three cars, or cuts of four cars or less, to stand on a sanded rail."

Traditionally, railroads have used storage batteries to provide the current for track circuits. Since a battery will experience constant drain when the track circuit remains clear, it is important to design a circuit with the lowest current draw to keep a relay energized while employing long-life batteries capable of maintaining a charge in a variety of atmospheric conditions. Track circuits use low voltage to minimize current leakage and to avoid the risk of electric shock to people and animals along the tracks.

A variety of primary batteries have been used for track circuits and signal operations, including caustic soda cells, nickel-cadmium cells, and lead-acid cells similar to those used in automobiles. Where external grid power is available, it is generally used to recharge batteries rather than power track circuits directly. This is done so that signals will continue to function if the external power is disrupted. If signal power should fail completely, failsafe rules demand that a malfunctioning signal must be observed as displaying its most restrictive aspect. If this is an absolute signal, it must be obeyed as an "absolute stop," and the train dispatcher will need to issue authority for a train to pass the signal.

🔊 In the 1970s, Southern Pacific began replacing US&S Style-B lower-quadrant semaphores on its Siskiyou Line in California. On February 18, 1979, semaphores remain in service at the east end of Hornbrook, but a pair of Raco color-light replacements have been installed. Although these Style-B signals feature blades with three lenses, they are designed only for two-position operation. The one-blade lower-quadrant signal seen here can display only "stop and proceed" and "clear" aspects. J. D. Schmid

RELAYS

A track circuit relay is a simple electromagnetic switch consisting of a wire coil wrapped around an iron core. When the coil is energized, it is magnetized, lifting an armature and completing one secondary electrical circuit. When the relay is de-energized, it drops, completing another secondary circuit. The relay is designed so that in the de-energized position, gravity acts on the armature to ensure it drops.

John Armstrong notes in his 1957 *TRAINS* article "All About Signals" that to avoid the possibility of a high-voltage electrical short welding the armature in an unsafe energized position, contacts are made from materials such as silver-impregnated graphite, which resists accidental welding. Further, the relay is sealed in glass, to protect moving parts. Despite technological advances that miniaturized many electrical components in other applications, track circuit relays remained bulky for many years, a result of their robustness. Relays used in track circuits must function reliably for years or decades with minimal attention.

While the simplest track circuit uses low-voltage direct current, in situations where electrical interference makes a basic DC track circuit impractical, polarized DC circuits and various forms of alternating-current track circuits can be used instead. One of the earliest applications of AC track circuits was on direct-current electric railways, where the rails returned the current and thus would disrupt a simple DC track circuit.

Every level of circuit complexity added to a signal system requires greater numbers of relays. A three-aspect block signal requires more complicated circuits than a basic two-aspect block signal, to transfer information of one circuit's condition to the next one. Approach lighting, block overlap, and AC track circuits each introduce a new level of circuit complexity.

Advanced signal systems that provide train control and/or cab signaling resulted in the development of coded track circuits, where information is passed through the rail in pulse codes. Different pulse rates indicate various signal

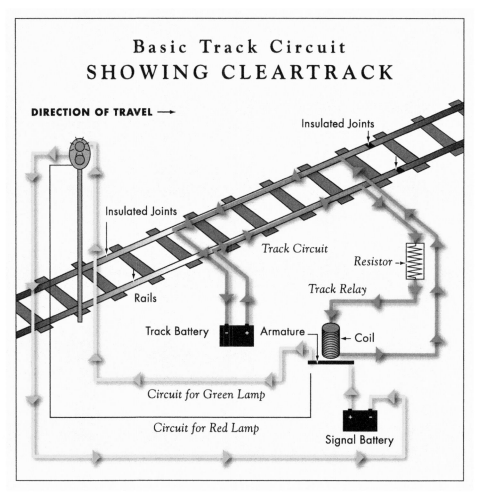

Basic Track Circuit
SHOWING CLEARTRACK

DIRECTION OF TRAVEL →

Insulated Joints

Insulated Joints

Track Circuit

Resistor →

Track Relay

Rails

Track Battery

Armature → ← Coil

Circuit for Green Lamp

Circuit for Red Lamp

Signal Battery

DIAGRAM 5.1   Diarmaid Collins / Rochelle Schultz

aspects. Traditionally, special circuits using pendulum relays generated pulse codes. Modern systems use solid-state electronics for coding. High-frequency track circuits are now used for many applications, including grade-crossing protection (see Chapter 8).

A standard safety feature afforded by a basic track circuit is the ability to detect an open switch. Switch points are wired into the track circuit so that if the switch is lined for the main route, the track circuit is undisturbed, and the signal will show "clear." However, if the switch is lined for a diverging route, the track circuit will be shunted, and the signal protecting the block will display "stop." In addition, a length of track on the diverging route approaching the switch can be wired into the track circuit so if railway equipment gets close to the switch and is in danger of fouling the mainline—causing an obstruction that could

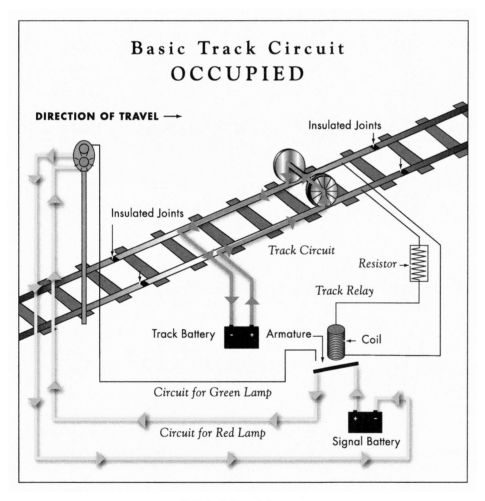

Basic Track Circuit
OCCUPIED

DIRECTION OF TRAVEL →

Insulated Joints

Insulated Joints

Track Circuit

Resistor →

Track Relay

Track Battery

Armature

← Coil

Circuit for Green Lamp

Circuit for Red Lamp

Signal Battery

Diarmaid Collins / Rochelle Schultz

DIAGRAM 5.2

interfere with a train—this equipment will shunt the circuit, causing the signal to display "stop."

Track circuits are also used to protect against misaligned switches. A facing point switch (facing the direction of traffic) can be especially dangerous. Even a slight deviation of the switch points can result in a derailment. A track circuit can be wired in conjunction with the

switch mechanism so that a misalignment of as little as 1/4 inch can shunt the track circuit to "stop."

AUTOMATIC BLOCK SIGNALS

Automatic block signaling offers a comparatively inexpensive method of providing space separation between trains. This system offers greater protection than afforded by traditional time separation and can also be used to increase line capacity while maintaining a high level of safety. The most effective automatic block systems use track circuits to indicate track occupancy and govern the control of line-side signals. A line is divided into sections (or blocks) of a specific length, each of which is an electrically isolated track circuit. In situations where a block is longer than practical for a single-track circuit, circuits can be linked together for the same basic effect.

The most basic application of the automatic block system features a signal that guards the entrance to a block and is controlled by the track circuit in that block. Assuming all equipment is functioning properly, when a train occupies the block, the track circuit in that block is shunted, causing the signal to display "stop." When the track is unoccupied, the signal will display "clear." Using this system, trains can safely follow one another over a line, moving from block to block, after the train in front has cleared. As with all basic signaling systems, it is up to the locomotive engineer to observe the signal aspects and adhere to the rules each signal indicates.

STOP AND PROCEED

Because an ABS system has the potential for signal failure and because signals are designed for failsafe operation, it is common in ABS territory to use the "stop and proceed" aspect in place of an absolute "stop" aspect (sometimes track on a line with directional double-track. Another example would be a single line where overlapping track circuits provide sufficient protection against the possibility of opposing movements (such as in an APB system, discussed in detail later).

The difference between a "stop" aspect and a "stop and proceed" aspect is extremely significant, since if an engineer

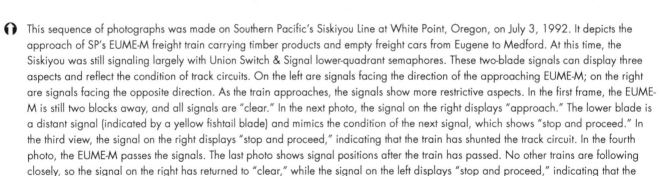

🔊 This sequence of photographs was made on Southern Pacific's Siskiyou Line at White Point, Oregon, on July 3, 1992. It depicts the approach of SP's EUME-M freight train carrying timber products and empty freight cars from Eugene to Medford. At this time, the Siskiyou was still signaling largely with Union Switch & Signal lower-quadrant semaphores. These two-blade signals can display three aspects and reflect the condition of track circuits. On the left are signals facing the direction of the approaching EUME-M; on the right are signals facing the opposite direction. As the train approaches, the signals show more restrictive aspects. In the first frame, the EUME-M is still two blocks away, and all signals are "clear." In the next photo, the signal on the right displays "approach." The lower blade is a distant signal (indicated by a yellow fishtail blade) and mimics the condition of the next signal, which shows "stop and proceed." In the third view, the signal on the right displays "stop and proceed," indicating that the train has shunted the track circuit. In the fourth photo, the EUME-M passes the signals. The last photo shows signal positions after the train has passed. No other trains are following closely, so the signal on the right has returned to "clear," while the signal on the left displays "stop and proceed," indicating that the block beyond this signal (behind the camera) is occupied. Brian Solomon

referred to as "stop and stay"). The "stop and proceed" aspect allows a train to continue after stopping rather than having to wait indefinitely at a malfunctioning signal. When a train encounters a "stop and proceed" signal, it is allowed to proceed only after stopping, and then at restricted speed—usually not more than 15 mph—and must expect to stop short of a train or obstruction within the block.

Often, the rules indicate that a train must not resume normal speed until after it has passed the next signal displaying a less restrictive aspect. The provision for "stop and proceed" can be applied safely in situations where traffic over a line operates only in one direction, such as a main

were to inadvertently mistake a "stop" for the less restrictive "stop and proceed," a collision could result. A fixed signal can display either "stop" or "stop and proceed" but not both, and the two types of fixed signals must be clearly distinguished from one another. A signal that displays "stop and proceed" can be considered a permissive signal, while one that displays "stop" is an absolute signal. (A permissive signal should not be confused with a "permissive" aspect. Some railroads, such as the Baltimore & Ohio, used signals that would display the latter—see the glossary.)

Absolute signals are used at the ends of controlled sidings, at junctions with other lines, and most other places where interlocking signals are required. Permissive signals are normally used in ABS territory between absolute signals and are often described as "intermediate" signals. Intermediate signals may control any number of blocks between absolutes.

The basic component of the "stop and proceed" aspect is often the same as a "stop" aspect, such as a horizontal semaphore blade or red color-light, so railroads must clearly distinguish between the types of fixed signal hardware

displaying these different aspects. Absolute signals are often distinguished by the lack of a number plate, while a permissive signal will carry a number plate on the signal mast. This follows failsafe practice: if a number plate falls off a permissive signal, it must be observed as the more restrictive absolute signal.

Additional elements may be incorporated in signal hardware design to make it easier to distinguish specific varieties of fixed signals. A standard system of semaphore blades in the U.S. consisted of the following practices: blades with squared-off ends were used for absolute (home) signals; solid red blades were used at interlockings; red blades with a white stripe on the end were used in automatic block territory; permissive signals used blades with pointed ends and a chevron stripe (depending on the rules of the individual railroad, these blades may have been painted yellow with a black chevron or red with a white chevron); and distant signals used yellow blades with a fishtail end and an inverted black chevron.

The backs of semaphores were often painted a neutral color, such as black, and sometimes featured a white stripe, to avoid confusing the back with the front. These standards had numerous exceptions. Santa Fe, for example, preferred semaphores with black blades with squared off ends in ABS

territory, presumably because black blades were easier to spot in the desert.

Some railways that used multiple-head color-light signals distinguished intermediate ABS signals by staggering the position of the heads on the mast. The top head was attached to the left-hand side of the mast and the lower head to the right. Color-position-light signals may use a marker lamp in conjunction with a pair of red lights in the horizontal position to indicate "stop and proceed." In all of these situations, number plates are still used to definitively distinguish permissive signals.

GRADE SIGNALS

In graded territory, some railroad rules allow freight trains to pass certain permissive signals displaying "stop and proceed" at restricted speed without stopping. This is allowed because of the impracticality of stopping a heavily laden freight train on a grade. In many instances, stopping such a train on a grade will incur a greater safety hazard than allowing it to keep moving, and get it moving again can prove difficult. It is preferable to allow a heavy freight to plod along at restricted speed prepared to stop but not stopping unless blocked by a train ahead.

These special signals are identified with a "G" or "P" printed on a yellow-orange colored marker plate. Sometimes they are known as "grade signals," although the rules that apply may be used in other circumstances where it is desirable to allow freight trains to crawl at restricted speed rather bringing them to a complete stop.

MULTIPLE-ASPECT AUTOMATIC BLOCK SIGNALS

Basic two-aspect automatic block limits traffic capacity and train speeds, especially in situations where blocks are

Three Aspect
AUTOMATIC BLOCK SYSTEM

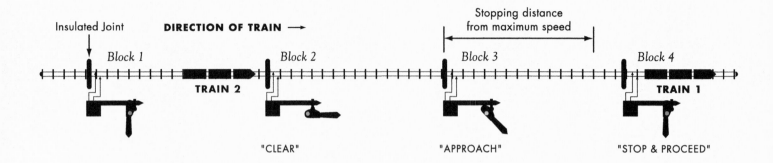

EACH BLOCK HAS AN INDEPENDENT TRACK CIRCUIT

DIAGRAM 5.3

Diarmaid Collins / Rochelle Schultz

quite long. A train has to approach each signal anticipating its most restrictive aspect and expect to stop. One of the simplest ways to improve train handling is to provide a distant signal to each absolute signal. The distant signal is positioned within stopping distance of the "home" absolute signal and mimics the condition of that signal, giving an engineer advance warning if he must stop. Although such systems are not common in the United States today, they were used in some of the earliest ABS installations and are common overseas, where blocks are very long.

To provide greater capacity, ABS signals may be evenly spaced, arranged so that each signal displays three aspects. Originally, this was done with lower-quadrant signals, where the top blade was an ABS home signal and the lower blade served as the distant signal, mimicking the condition of the next ABS home signal. (In this example, "home" does not imply an "absolute" signal but rather one that shows "clear" or "stop and proceed," while a distant shows "clear" or "caution"/"approach.") With the introduction of three-aspect upper-quadrant signaling, the aspects were organized so that the middle aspect indicated "approach," conveying the information that the next signal was displaying "stop" or "stop and proceed."

Some railroads use the "approach" aspect with speed signaling. While the basic meaning conveyed by "approach" is the same, the instructions for how to interpret the aspect have become more explicit. For example, the NORAC rules

for an "approach" aspect specify, "Proceed prepared to stop at the next signal. Trains exceeding Medium Speed must begin reduction to Medium Speed as soon as the engine passes the Approach signal."

Signal spacing is based on the required braking distance between ABS signals. The failure to lower a train's speed in preparation for stopping as soon as the signal is passed may result in the train overrunning the next signal if it displays a "stop" aspect. Using speed aspects dictates a specific action to locomotive engineers.

One method of increasing track capacity is to place blocks closer together. The more closely blocks are spaced, the more closely trains can follow one another with proper signal protection. A train must be able to stop safely when it receives an "approach" aspect, and block length must accommodate the distance required to bring a train under control using normal braking measures, while leaving some a margin for error.

The minimum block length depends on the weight and speed of the trains operating over the line. On rapid transit lines, where trains are relatively light, short, operate at slow speeds, and require close headways between runs, block length can be short. Rapid transit blocks are often only a few hundred feet in length. However, on railroad mainlines, where heavy trains are operating at relatively high speeds, blocks must be much longer.

If a railroad wants to increase train speed, it may be

faced with a situation where block lengths are too short to allow faster trains to stop safely. It has several choices: it can respace signals to create longer blocks, improve the braking of its trains to conform with existing signal spacing, or modify signaling to include a fourth aspect.

The first option can be expensive, as a railroad will need to relocate signal hardware. This option also poses operational constraints if the railroad is running a mix of

The second option, improving braking, is uncommon. One prominent example is the British Rail HST (High Speed Train). In the mid-1970s, BR speeded up long-distance passenger service by using pairs of high-powered diesels in a push-pull configuration on each consist, giving enough power to accelerate quickly to 125 mph, significantly faster than existing traffic. While a few lines were modified for very fast running, one of the advantages of the

(U) Amtrak's *Lake Shore Limited* rolls west at Hammond-Whiting, Indiana, having just crossed from the former New York Central to the former Pennsylvania. The PRR used its famous position-light signals, such as those pictured here. The two outer signals display "stop" aspects, while the center signal displays "approach medium," indicating that the next signal displays "medium clear." PRR position-lights mimic the aspects used by semaphores. Brian Solomon

(U) The center signal displays "slow approach." Under NORAC this is Rule 288, which states, "Proceed prepared to stop at next signal. Slow Speed applies until train clears all interlocking or spring switches, then Medium Speed applies." This signal can be displayed with color lights using red over red over flashing yellow. (See Diagram 5-3.)

train types. While faster trains will be allowed greater stopping distance, some slower-moving trains will receive approach signals before they need them, causing them to slow unnecessarily, increasing travel time while reducing line capacity. On a heavily traveled line, introducing capacity constraints may be undesirable and counterproductive.

Some railroads overcame these difficulties by using multiple track. In the steam era, New York Central operated a four-track mainline, where one pair of tracks was intended for passenger trains and some fast freights, while the other pair was used for slower-moving traffic, especially slow freights.

HST design was that it used modern braking systems to slow more effectively than conventional trains, allowing it stop safely within existing signaling spacing.

The third option is accomplished by introducing more blocks and more signal aspects. By providing three blocks protection, an engineer is given two blocks warning of a stop signal, which effectively doubles the distance available to slow his train. A fourth aspect is needed to show the condition of tracks three blocks ahead, an arrangement known as four-aspect three-block signaling. It successfully accommodates the braking requirements of fast-moving trains—where greater distance is required to stop—while minimizing the delay to slower-moving trains. It can also be used to reduce delays for traffic running at close headways or where trains need to stop frequently, such as on a commuter line.

To better understand benefits of a four-aspect, three-block system, here is a real-life example: In 1935, Chicago & North Western resignaled a portion of its Chicago and Milwaukee double-track mainline via Wilmette, Illinois, and St. Francis, Wisconsin. (C&NW operated two mainlines between Chicago and Milwaukee.) This was the primary route for its famous high-speed "400" passenger trains that connected Chicago with St. Paul/Minneapolis in 400 minutes. The old signal system, consisting of two-aspect Hall disc signals, could not effectively accommodate the mixed need for high-speed running and frequent Chicago-area suburban traffic.

An article by S. E. Noble, assistant signal engineer for the C&NW, in the November 1935 *Railway Signaling*, described the circumstances facing C&NW. The Hall signals had been in place for about 30 years, and C&NW carefully considered its signaling needs before replacing the existing system. At rush hours, suburban passenger trains followed one another closely in and out of Chicago. C&NW offered both local and express trains, which resulted in traffic congestion, especially during morning rush hour, when trains converged on Chicago. At times of peak traffic, trains were scheduled on 3-minute headways. In addition, the 400s were allowed to operate at speeds between 80 and 95 mph (depending on track condition). Noble examines the specifics of the situation:

Calculated stopping distances and tests indicated that for these speeds, signals of a three-aspect, two-block system would have to be spaced 7,000 to 8,000 ft. apart if it were desired to stop a train without making an emergency [brake] application. The old overlap system, previously in use,

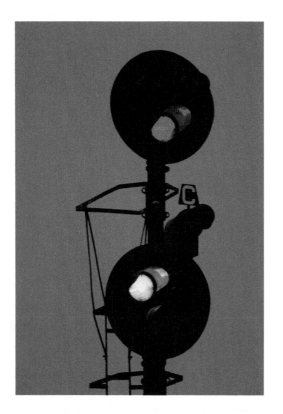

The westward signal at Palmer, Massachusetts, displays red over yellow, a "restricting" aspect, NORAC Rule 290. The former Boston & Albany is now cab signal territory, and the "C" light between the two main heads can be used to display a "clear to next interlocking" aspect, Rule 280A. This aspect authorizes a train without an operative cab signal receiver to proceed to the next fixed signal and is necessary where there are no intermediate signals. Brian Solomon

caused innumerable stops during the rush hour on account of the length of the overlap. Although a three-aspect two-block system would probably eliminate some of the stops, it would still cause considerable delay due to the C&NW Rule 501B for an approach signal [aspect], requiring a train exceeding 30 m.p.h. to at once reduce to that speed. Spacing of 7,000 to 8,000 ft. would cause more than one suburban station to fall within a block, and the benefit of a nearby signal in protecting a station stop would be lost.

Noble explains that the most logical solution was the installation of a four-aspect, three-block system. Block lengths between Wilmette and Highland Park varied in length from 2,996 feet to 6,600 feet, depending on the location of the passenger stations. The inbound track used a four-aspect, three-block system the entire distance from Highland Park to Wilmette (where the railroad expanded to a three-track line). The outbound track mixed four-aspect, three-block and three-aspect, two block systems, as appropriate for the station spacing.

The design of this signal system took into consideration other factors, such as low fog that occurs regularly along Lake Michigan, and C&NW's unconventional practice of left-hand running. Signal hardware consisted of a mix of Type-D color-light signals and searchlight signals. Signals were generally mounted on masts rather than on overhead bridges.

DISPLAYING FOUR-ASPECT SIGNALS

A fourth aspect may be displayed in a variety of ways, depending on individual railway practices. In American practice, the fourth aspect is placed between "clear" and "approach." Alternatively the fourth aspect could be placed ahead of the "clear" aspect, providing an "advance clear," but this practice has generally been frowned upon, because it would require a signal less restrictive than "clear," which may cause confusion.

On lines that use speed signaling, the fourth aspect can be provided with "approach medium" or "advance approach." "Approach medium" is typically displayed with color-light signals as a yellow over green. Upper-quadrant semaphore and position-light signals can both display

On Christmas Day 1991, Chicago & North Western SD60 8013 leads an empty unit coal train, symbol PPROX, destined for Wyoming's Powder River Basin, below a signal bridge at Elmhurst, Illinois. When C&NW improved its Chicago-Omaha mainline between Elmhurst and West Chicago in 1924–25, it added a third mainline track, which it signaled for bidirectional operation. For this project, C&NW worked with GRS to develop a horizontal color-light signal. C&NW believed the color light was most effective if the height of the signal could be reduced. As a result, this unusual color-light configuration has been a distinctive feature of C&NW Chicago-area lines for almost 80 years. Another unusual C&NW practice is left-hand running, contrary to typical North American operation. Mike Abalos

"approach medium" with a 45-degree diagonal over a vertical (this equates directly with yellow over green). Using a color-position-light system, "approach medium" is displayed by a pair of vertical green lights and a white marker lamp located above and to the left of the signal head. (This system displays "clear" with a pair of vertical green lights

107

⌒ Signals must be placed so that crews have optimal viewing of the heads. This photo was made on the Southern Pacific in the Oregon Cascades west of Frazier, at the east portal of Tunnel 13 on June 13, 1994. Notice that the right-hand searchlight is sharply angled to be visible for westbound trains coming through the tight curve. The box to the left of the tracks contains signal relays. Brian Solomon

and a white marker lamp directly above the signal head.) The progression of aspects (from least to most restrictive) in a three-block, four aspect system using "approach medium" would be "clear," "approach medium," "approach," "stop."

NORAC rules for the "approach medium" indication state, "Proceed approaching next signal at Medium Speed." This rule gives a slower-moving train flexibility, allows it to continue traveling at track speed until it approaches the next signal, and does not mandate an immediate speed reduction. "Approach medium" can also be used to indicate that the next signal is displaying "medium clear."

The "advance approach" indication can be used in conjunction with either speed or route signaling and may be displayed by a either a flashing yellow aspect or a double yellow aspect.

Southern Pacific uses flashing yellow and assigns it Rule 234, which defines "advance approach" as follows: "Proceed prepared to stop at second signal unless the next signal displays a Clear, Approach Diverging or Advance Approach aspect." The latter portion of this rule is significant, because if a train is following two blocks behind another, it may repeatedly encounter "advance approach" aspects unless the spacing between the trains changes or the preceding train takes a diverging route.

An advantage of the "advance approach" is that it offers a fourth aspect (flashing yellow) with color-light signaling without requiring a second signal head. Thus, a railroad can easily convert an existing three-aspect, two-block ABS system that uses single-head color-lights into a four-aspect, three-block system by using additional relay circuits. A traditional flashing signal displays a "slow stately flash" and not the rapid blinking associated with common highway signals. Southern Pacific even adapted its lower-quadrant semaphores to display "advance approach" with the addition of a flashing yellow light below the semaphore blades.

"Advance approach" can be applied to speed signaling, and NORAC Rule 282a give the aspect the following indication: "Proceed prepared to stop at the second signal. Trains exceeding Limited Speed must begin reduction to Limited Speed as soon as engine passes the Advance Approach signal."

The double yellow (yellow over yellow) is a less common way of displaying advanced approach in the United States but is widely used as a fourth aspect in British practice, in which the normal meanings for color-light signals are that red indicates "Danger"—stop; yellow indicates "Caution"—proceed prepared to stop at the next signal; and green indicates "All right" or "clear"—expect next signal to exhibit "Caution" or "clear." Under this system, two yellow lights, one over the other, indicates "Warning"—proceed and be prepared to pass the next signal at "Caution."

In the United States, a double yellow signal can be assigned other indications, usually in conjunction with interlocking signals, and may be far more restrictive than either "approach" or "approach medium." For example, many Western railroads use double yellow for "approach diverging." In this case, the signal is not used for three-block protection but to indicate that the next signal is "diverging" and that the train should expect to take a switch for a diverging route or siding.

On St. Patrick's Day 1983, an outbound Chicago & North Western passenger train passes below the signal bridge at Noble Street in Chicago. This view portrays the back of GRS Model 2A semaphores protecting the tracks for inbound moves. Each signal is centered over the track it protects. The four aspects displayed from left to right are "clear," "approach," "stop," and "approach." The signal bridge in the distance displays an "approach" for this train; the other signals display "clear." Mike Abalos

SIGNAL LOCATION

The spacing and location of fixed signals must be designed to give locomotive engineers the best possible sighting. Locating signals on straight track in open country is fairly straightforward. Provided there are no unusual operating conditions, signals are spaced at even intervals based solely on braking distances, and with right-hand running they are positioned on signal masts to the right of the track, facing the locomotive. Ideally, the height of a signal is set for easy sighting from the locomotive cab. For example, a typical Pennsylvania Railroad 4061 single-head position-light signal was placed on a mast with the center of the top head 17 feet above the ground. If a second head were required, this would have been centered 5 feet below the center of the top head.

SIGNAL BRIDGES

In many situations, it is impractical to locate a signal immediately adjacent to the right-hand side of the track it governs. There are several options. On a single-track line, a signal can be placed on the left-hand side of the tracks, traditionally known as the "fireman's" side, because on

Chesapeake & Ohio's "A" Tower at Allegheny Summit, Virginia, looking east on October 9, 1947. Cantilever signal bridges placed the Union Switch & Signal color-lights over the tracks they governed. Bruce Fales; Jay Williams collection

American lines the fireman rode on the left-hand side of the locomotive. This is done when space considerations prevent the preferred location of a signal on the right-hand side.

In the days of steam power, a locomotive engineer had limited sighting, since he had to peer through a comparatively small window, with the mass of the locomotive boiler obscuring much of his view. Because of this, left-hand placement was generally frowned upon, since it would have been

difficult for an engineer to spot the signal. However, modern diesels offer an excellent forward view when operated normally, so in modern installations, signals on the left-hand side pose less difficulty. (Obviously, a locomotive running long hood forward will still face limited sighting.) As an economy move, some railways have routinely placed signals for both directions back to back on a common mast.

A better placement option is on overhead signal bridges. When this is done, a signal should be situated directly over the right-hand rail of the track it governs. Signal bridges are routinely used on lines with three or more tracks and in places where it may be desirable to signal a double-track line in both directions.

A great variety of signal bridge styles has been used over the years. A full-span lattice steel bridge was a traditional choice. A few lines, such as New York Central, Santa Fe, and Southern Pacific, used cantilever signal bridges, especially on single-track lines where an unsignaled siding or spur was located directly to the right of the mainline track. A cantilever bridge is also useful where a tall signal is required for better sighting or where a tall signal will be plagued by high winds.

A standard Santa Fe cantilever bridge reaching over an unsignaled track featured a single mast positioned 7 feet 9 inches to the right of the right-hand rail of the unsignaled track. The bridge was just over 23 feet tall, with the signal mounted on top of a horizontal section extending 16 feet to the left over both tracks. In rare instances, signals may be mounted on other types of overhead structures, such as highway overpasses or pedestrian footbridges.

A common arrangement at large terminals with many tracks is to use long bridges with a multitude of signals, each governing a specific track. It may be difficult for a locomotive engineer to pick out the specific signal that governs the track his train is running on, so the signals may have numbers that correspond to the track they govern.

SIGNAL MASTS

In double-track territory, some railways use tall masts with a bracket at the top to hold a pair of signals adjacent to one another. Assuming there are two tracks, the left-hand signal will govern the left-hand track, while the right-hand governs the right-hand track. New York Central used this arrangement on its lines west of Buffalo; originally, the

Northeast Operating Rules Advisory Committee – 7th Edition

COLOR LIGHT
INTERLOCKING & ABS SIGNALS

NAME	ASPECT	INDICATION
CLEAR	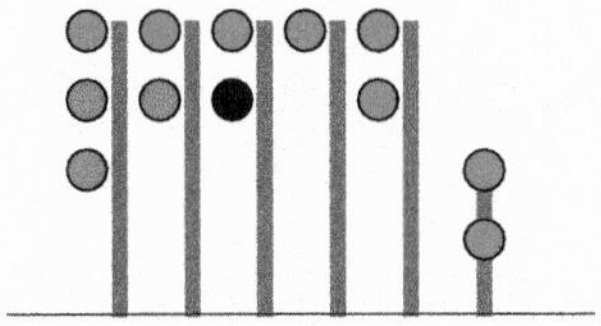	**Rule 280** Proceed not exceeding Normal Speed.
CAB SPEED	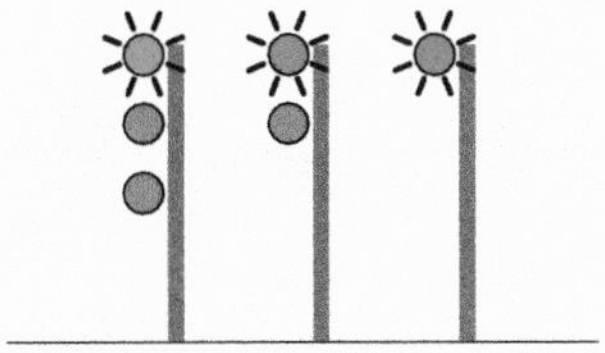	**Rule 281-A** Proceed in accordance with cab signal indication. Reduce speed to not exceeding 60 mph if Cab Speed cab signal is displayed without a signal speed, or if cab signals are not operative.
APPROACH LIMITED	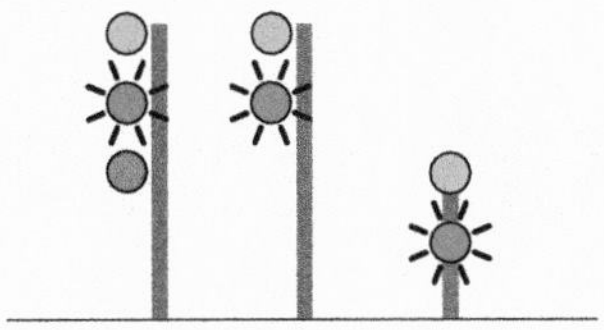	**Rule 281-B** Proceed approaching the next signal at limited speed.
LIMITED CLEAR	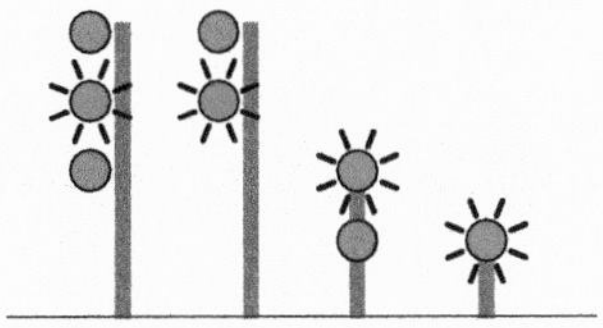	**Rule 281-C** Proceed at Limited Speed until entire train clears all interlocking or spring switches, then proceed at Normal Speed. [Additional information applies in cab signal territory.]
APPROACH MEDIUM	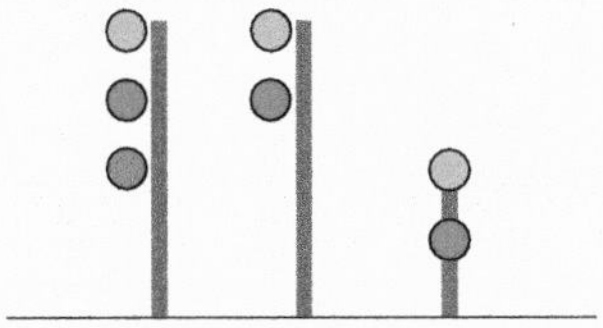	**Rule 282** Proceed approaching the next signal at medium speed.
ADVANCE APPROACH	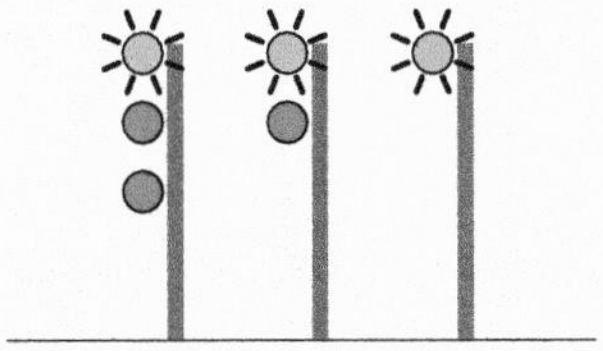	**Rule 282-A** Proceed prepared to stop at the second signal. Trains exceeding Limited Speed must begin reduction to Limited Speed as soon as engine passes the Advance Approach signal.
MEDIUM CLEAR	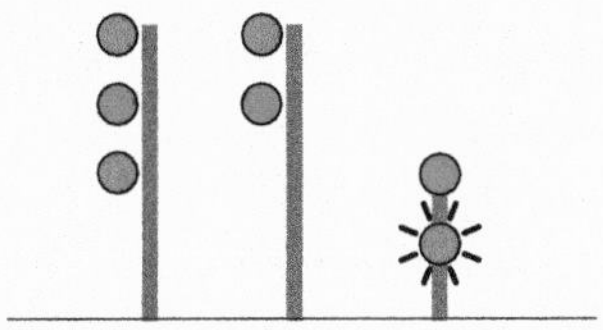	**Rule 283** Proceed at Medium Speed until entire train clears all interlocking or spring switches, then proceed at Normal Speed. [Additional information applies in cab signal territory.]
MEDIUM APPROACH MEDIUM	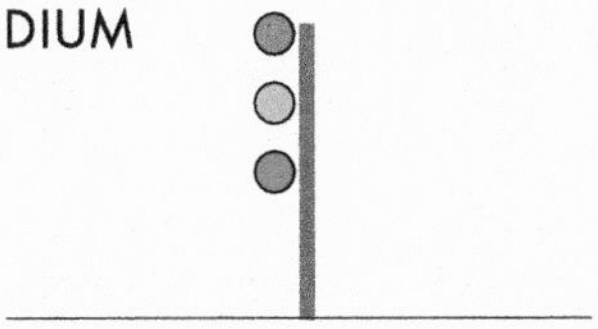	**Rule 283-A** Proceed at maximum speed until entire train clears all interlocking or spring switches, then approach the next signal at Medium Speed. Trains exceeding Medium Speed must begin reduction to Medium Speed as soon as the Medium Approach Medium signal is clearly visible.

Diarmaid Collins / Rochelle Schultz

DIAGRAM 5.4

NAME	ASPECT	INDICATION
APPROACH SLOW		**Rule 284** Proceed approaching the next signal at Slow Speed. Trains exceeding Medium Speed must begin reduction to Medium Speed as soon as the engine passes the Approach Slow signal.
APPROACH		**Rule 285** Proceed prepared to stop at the next signal. Trains exceeding Medium Speed must begin reduction to Medium Speed as soon as the engine passes the Approach signal.
MEDIUM APPROACH		**Rule 286** Proceed prepared to stop at the next signal. Trains exceeding Medium Speed must begin reduction to Medium Speed as soon as the Medium Approach signal is clearly visible.
SLOW CLEAR		**Rule 287** Proceed at Slow Speed until entire train clears all interlocking or spring switches, then proceed at Normal Speed. [Additional information applies in cab signal territory.]
SLOW APPROACH		**Rule 288** Proceed prepared to stop at next signal. Slow speed applies until entire train clears all interlocking or spring switches, then proceed at Normal Speed. [Additional information applies in cab signal territory.]
RESTRICTING		**Rule 290** Proceed at Restricted Speed until the entire train has cleared all interlocking and spring switches (if signal is an interlocking or Control Point signal) and the leading wheels have: passed a more favorable fixed signal, or entered non-signal Form D Control System territory [Additional information applies in cab signal territory.]
STOP & PROCEED		**Rule 291** Stop, then proceed at Restricted Speed until the entire train has cleared all interlocking and spring switches (if signal is an interlocking or Control Point signal) & the leading wheels have passed a more favorable fixed signal, or entered non-signal Form D Control System territory. [Additional information applies in cab signal territory, & where a letter G or letter R marker is displayed.]
STOP SIGNAL		**Rule 292** Stop

DIAGRAM 5.4a

Diarmaid Collins / Rochelle Schultz

signals carried Hall lower-quadrant semaphores and, later GRS color-lights. Erie Railroad used such signal masts on its double-track lines.

In unusual situations, where a signal mast is located to the right of tracks and where an unsignaled track sits to the right of the track a signal governs, a dummy post will be located to the right of the signal, indicating that it governs the track to the right rather than the track adjacent to the signal. Some railroads place a marker lamp on such a post, typically a fixed blue light. In rare situations where two unsignaled tracks sit between the signal mast and the main track, two marker posts or lamps will sit to the right of the signal.

↻ It's May 1976, and a morning Amtrak train, led by a brand new Electro-Motive F40PH-2, heads toward New Haven. In the distance are the John Hancock towers. Pictured are former New Haven left-handed semaphores, located on a gantry near Boston's Back Bay Station. The signal on the right governs the right-hand main track; the signal on the left govern the next track over. Both signals show green over red, "clear." Fred Matthews

BLOCK SIGNAL PLACEMENT

Normally, a block signal is positioned in front of the block it protects, so the train will be stopped before it enters the block. Signal placement must take into consideration where a train will stop. The limits of the block may need to be adjusted to accommodate a variety of special situations, such as the location of stations, highway crossings, bridges, and sharp curves. Signal locations will be arranged so that trains do not unnecessarily block road crossings. For this reason, it is quite common to find ABS signals located just short of road crossings. This has the added advantage of making a stopped train more accessible to the highway, which can be useful if railway personnel need to reach a train for maintenance or a crew change.

Signals located on curves may need taller masts and adjusted head angles to improve visibility. In some situations, where especially sharp curves or obstructions make sighting a signal difficult, a repeater signal may be provided that mimics the indication of the primary block signal. Such a signal must be clearly identified, so that it will not be confused with the primary block signal. Repeater signals are rarely used in North America but are common in Britain. Where an overhead bridge may obstruct the view of a signal, a short mast may be used. However, an ABS signal with a short mast should not be confused with a dwarf signal—a ground signal used at interlockings and sidings.

ABS AT WORK

In a basic ABS system, signals are wired to protect against following movements. As a train passes from block to block, signals behind it protect the rear of the train by warning following trains. The signal guarding an occupied block will show "stop," and as the train proceeds in the next block, the signal will clear to "approach," and then to "clear" when the train reaches the second block. If one were to observe a semaphore (or a continuously lit color-light automatic block signal) facing against the direction of travel of an approaching train on single-track, it would drop in the reverse order as the train entered each successive block. So, looking toward an oncoming train, the signal will display "clear" as long as the train is least two blocks away, then "approach" when it is just one block away, and then "stop" when the train has entered the block. As soon as the train passes the signal and has exited the block, if no other trains are following within two blocks, the ABS signal should immediately return to "clear."

A problem with the basic system is that the signals do not provide sufficient protection for opposing movements on single-track, so another system of control must be in place to assure that trains do not collide head-on. In North America, trains can be authorized by a controlled signal (such as an interlocking signal) or by an established form of written authorization. Traditionally, written authority was conveyed by timetable and train order instructions; today written authority may be conveyed in the form of Direct Traffic Control block authority, track warrant, or Form D. This authority is often transmitted verbally by radio (see Chapter 6). Contemporary NORAC rules read:

Automatic Block Signal (ABS) Rules apply only where designated by Timetable or Bulletin Order. Their purpose is to control the movement of trains in territory where the entrance to each block is governed by fixed signals, cab signals, or both. ABS signals convey to trains the occupancy and/or condition of track ahead of them. Under normal conditions train movements are authorized by these signals.

Although this last sentence may appear contradictory in regards to the authorization of train movements, it has been made clear in NORAC rules that a train must have authority to enter ABS territory, and once that authority has been conveyed, then ABS signals convey authority to proceed. NORAC Rule 500 reads,

A train must not enter or foul ABS territory without a proceed indication on a controlled signal or verbal permission of the Dispatcher (or Operator when authorized by the Dispatcher). When verbal permission is given to enter Rule 261 territory, the permission must include an authorized direction of movement.

Directional double-track that permits trains to proceed on signal indication is handled under Rule 251. A traditional definition of Rule 251, as prescribed by the *Standard Code* revised in 1938, states, "On portions of the railroad, and on designated tracks so specified on the time-table, trains will run with reference to other trains in the same direction by block signals whose indications will supersede the superiority of trains."

In modern operations, the traditional timetable and train order rules involving the superiority of trains has been largely dispensed with, and new interpretations of Rule 251 have been defined. For example, in the 7th edition

NORAC rulebook, effective January 2000, Rule 251 is defined: "When track is signaled in only one direction, signal indication will be the authority for trains to operate with the current of traffic. Movements against the current of traffic will be governed by non-signaled DCS rules [Form D control system]."

Within the limits of 251 territory, there may be sidings, spurs, and crossovers with switches that can be operated manually. Since these switches are tied into the track circuit and the normal position is lined for the mainline, the reversal of a switch will be protected by the block signal system. Authority to operate switches must be conveyed by the dispatcher. A common feature of 251 territory is manually operated trailing point crossovers. Such crossovers allow a train to cross from one line to the other only by reversing direction on the main track. This limits the potential for a head on-collision caused by the misalignment of facing point switches.

Double-track lines equipped with block signals in both directions are usually governed by Rule 261, which is basically the same as Rule 251, except that it permits the movement of trains by signal indication over either line in either direction.

ABSOLUTE PERMISSIVE BLOCK

In a basic single-track ABS system, if two trains were to head toward one another at equal speeds separated by two full blocks, both trains could conceivably receive "clear" aspects and then reach the end of their respective blocks simultaneously, facing red signals and one another. In such a situation, it is quite possible the trains would have neither the time nor the space to stop safely, resulting in a head-on collision.

One solution to this problem, using three-aspect, two-block signaling, was to provide an overlap in the track circuits, giving trains successive "approach" aspects to warn of traffic ahead. In a situation where trains are opposing one another, this would give engineers time to act and safely stop their trains with time and space to spare.

The drawback of overlapping track circuits is that with basic track circuitry, the direction of travel cannot be determined, and overlaps greatly lengthen the zone of protection

behind a train, limiting capacity for following moves. This was the difficulty that C&NW faced on its Chicago to Milwaukee line in the earlier example.

Another difficulty is that the zone of protection may not be coordinated with passing sidings, so while safety is provided, in the event of a misread order, two trains may occupy single-track face to face without anyplace to pass.

The development of Absolute Permissive Block provided a neat solution to this problem. It used sophisticated relay circuits to detect the direction of travel and thus set the signals to allow maximum capacity for following moves with maximum safety for opposing moves. Using a mix of absolute and permissive ABS signals, APB permits closely spaced following moves, allowing trains to move from block to block in the normal fashion governed by a two-block ABS system. At the same time, APB provides sufficient separation between opposing moves to safely avoid head-on collisions while automatically stopping trains at designated passing sidings.

Under normal circumstances, APB signaling, like other forms of ABS, is used in conjunction with another form of

track authority, so the signals do not actually authorize train movements but simply offer greater protection. When signals solely authorize train movements, it is clearly defined in a company's rules. APB signals are designed to protect against misread train orders and the inadvertent issuing of overlapping authority that could place two trains on a collision course. But a train must still have authority to operate before it can proceed in APB territory.

In the basic APB system, absolute signals are used at the ends of blocks that have a passing siding with switches at both ends. Permissive signals are between sidings. The

115

circuits are wired to detect the direction of travel using stick relay circuits. (GRS defines a stick relay as one "circuited so that it can be kept energized—once picked up—through its own front contact.") When a train proceeds into the block, it passes an absolute signal at the end of a siding, which sets a relay circuit putting all the opposing signals to stop between that siding and the next (in the direction of travel). This includes the absolute signal at the end of the next siding section. In this way, a train can safely proceed to the next block section, even if another train is holding on the main track or proceeding against it from the far side of the siding.

The two siding sections can have any number of intermediate signals between them. The signals behind the moving train will automatically clear in the normal ABS fashion, allowing following trains to maintain close headways.

To demonstrate how the Absolute Permissive Block system works, we will use an example featuring two trains on a section of track with three sidings: Able, Baker, and Charlie.

In all of these APB scenarios, signals are operated strictly by the track circuits. The signals are automatic and reflect the condition of the track circuits. There are no automatic switches—all of the switches are manually lined by members of the train crews. The position of the switches affects the circuitry, allowing trains to follow signal indications to pass one another safely. In addition, all the events have been predetermined by the appropriate form of track authority, be that timetable, train order, or modern radio authorization.

Train "101" is southbound, and "202" is northbound. To start the first example, Train 202 is at Able siding and train 101 is at Charlie siding. They are proceeding toward one another for a scheduled meet at intermediate Baker siding.

In scenario number 1, train 101 reaches Baker before 202 passes the northward absolute signal at Able. According to 101's orders, it takes the siding at Baker and restores the switches to the normal position for the mainline. Since 202 has not yet entered the circuits that affect the blocks between Able and Baker, 101 sees only green signals on its southward trip between Charlie and Baker. No other southbound trains are following 101 between Baker and Charlie, and if the circuits are functioning properly, the northward

ABS signals will all indicate "clear," allowing train 202 to pass 101 at Baker unhindered.

Because this is APB territory, when 202 passes the northward absolute signal at the north end of Able, all the opposing signals between Able and Baker will simultaneously drop from "clear" to "stop" rather than gradually dropping from "clear" to "approach" to "stop" in advance of the train, as would be the case in normal automatic block territory.

Once 202 is entirely clear of the south switch of Baker, and assuming no other trains are following 202 between Baker and Able, all the southward signals between these two points will show clear, and the crew of train 101 can manually reverse the south switch, lining it for the siding, and proceed south. (The crew at the tail end of the train will have to restore the siding switch to normal by manually re-lining it for the mainline once the entire train is out of the siding.) If there were a second northbound train south of Able, it would automatically face restrictive ("approach") aspects on approach to Able and a "stop" aspect at the north end of Able as soon as 101 passes the southward absolute signal at Baker.

In the second scenario, the basic conditions are essentially the same: 101 has taken the siding at Baker, and the mainline is clear behind it between Baker and Charlie. However, in this case, there are two northbound trains, 202 and 204, following two blocks apart. After 202 passes the southward signal at Baker, the signal remains in the full "stop" position, even though 204 is still two blocks away. This signal will show "stop" because 204 has entered the track circuit north of the north switch of Able. This would be true whether Able and Baker were separated by two blocks or by twenty. Once 204 has passed the south switch at Baker, and assuming no other trains are following between Baker and Able, 101 will again be able to continue as in the previous scenario.

In a third scenario, trains 101 and 202 are approaching Baker at roughly equal speeds, from Charlie and Able, respectively. Northward train 202 will receive "clear" signals until it reaches the distant signal to Baker, located one full block south of the south switch of the siding. This signal will display "approach," mandating the engineer to immediately reduce to "medium speed" —defined by this railroad's rules as 30 mph—and be prepared to stop at the next signal. When the train reaches the southward signal at

Baker, this signal also displays "approach," allowing 202 to continue on the mainline until it reaches the northward signal—an absolute signal, displaying "stop."

As 202 is passing the distant signal to the south end of Baker, 101 is approaching the distant signal to the north end of Baker, which also displays "approach." This signal has displayed "approach" since 202 passed the northward absolute signal at Able. If 202 had lined into the siding and was in the clear of the main track before 101 reached the distant to the north end of Baker, this signal would have cleared to "clear." However, train 202 will hold the mainline, and train 101 has orders to take the siding at Baker.

As 101 approaches the north end of Baker preparing to stop, 202 is easing up to the northward absolute signal. The two trains are facing each other a hundred feet apart. The crew of 202 lines the north switch at Baker, to allow 101 to take the siding. When this is done, 101, having stopped, can then pass the southward signal at the north end of Baker, which is displaying "stop and proceed." The meet between the two trains is complete.

These same meets could have been made on single-track without signals or with a basic ABS system, relying entirely on train orders (or, in modern times, radio authority) to establish the order of events. With APB, the signals ensure a greater level of protection for the meet without impairing the progress of either train. With APB, if train 202 had misread its meet order with 101 at Baker, it still would have encountered aspects on approach to Baker. Obeying these signal indications would have prevented a collision.

Normally in APB territory, a telephone is located at every absolute signal. This phone is wired directly to the dispatcher's office, allowing a train to request further instructions, report malfunctioning signals, or obtain other operational information.

The actual wiring of APB signals varies, depending on specifics of the line they are protecting. Some railroads preferred to give trains two successive "approach" aspects when approaching a siding where a meet was to take place. Other lines used special auxiliary signal heads to indicate that a train should take a siding. This could be a separate semaphore blade, disc signal, or a light.

The ability of trains to follow from block to block while being given absolute protection from opposing movements allowed APB intermediate signals to work as grade signals. As explained earlier, grade signals carry a special plate that allows heavy trains to pass them at restricted speed without stopping when they display "stop and proceed." This would apply strictly to permissive signals and by no means to the absolute signals at the ends of sidings.

On modern American railroads, APB systems have largely given way to various forms of Centralized Traffic

Railroads install auxiliary signals for special types of protection. This signal along the Milwaukee Road at Boylston, Washington, warned of high wind conditions on the Columbia River Bridge at Beverly. At times, the wind across this bridge could exceed 100 mph, fast enough to cause problems for freight trains. Normally, the signal was lit (some sources say flashing yellow), indicating that conditions on the bridge were safe. When an anemometer on the bridge detected wind speed over 60 mph, the signal would display no light (dark). The signal was wired separately from the track circuit and the information carried on the line wire. J. D. Schmid

Control. Yet many lines still use APB signaling, particularly in the Midwest and Far Western states. Understanding the principles behind APB will help in understanding the working of CTC systems, as the development of CTC was an outgrowth of APB. The two systems use similar relay circuits.

CENTRALIZED TRAFFIC CONTROL

REMOTE MEETING ON DESERT SIDING

The silhouette of distant mountains looms against the fading glow of the setting sun, while on a lonely, single-track desert mainline, all appears quiet. Here, the twin-head searchlight home signal that guards the westward entrance to a remote passing siding is dark. Then, as the stars begin to glimmer in the evening sky, a relay box across from the home signal comes alive. Banks of relays start ticking, communicating vital information sent from a dispatching desk more than a thousand miles away. As the last daylight fades on the horizon, the distant droning of Electro-Motive diesels rolls across the desert floor, announcing the approach of a fast-moving westbound freight.

Minutes later, the approach-lit signal lights up, displaying yellow over red—an "approach" aspect. Finally, the headlights of the westbound illuminate the home signal as the whine of dynamic brakes and the hiss of train air indicate the westbound is slowing. Its locomotives ease pass the eastward home signal with more than a mile of freight cars in tow.

Soon after the last car passes, the flashing of the end-of-train device intermittently lights the back of the signal. Once these cars are in the clear of the east siding switch and eastward signals, the switch reverses, meaning the points slide over, lining a new route from the siding to the mainline. The siding signal clears to display red over green—"diverging"—allowing an eastbound train crawling at restricted speed through the siding to pass the signal and enter the mainline.

A few more minutes pass, and the eastbound rolls out of the siding. The westbound, having received a clear signal at the west switch of the siding, pulls forward. Soon, both trains are rolling away from one another on the mainline at speed. The signals are again dark, and the relay box quiet.

Zane is a remote desert siding in southwest Utah, on Union Pacific's Los Angeles & Salt Lake Route. A westbound rolls past the east switch at Lund to make a meet with an eastbound. Switches and signals are controlled from hundreds of miles away, in Omaha, Nebraska. **Above:** Twilight view of the east switch of the Zane siding. UP's standard siding length on this route is 6,000 to 6,200 feet long, and according to UP's timetable, Zane is 6,006 feet. By the late 1940s, UP had approximately 650 miles of CTC in operation between Salt Lake City and Los Angeles, making for one of the longest lines under CTC control at that time. Brian Solomon

Similar scenes happen hundreds of times every day on modern single-track mainline railways all over North America. The settings vary from mountains to plains and forest, but the basics remain the same. This is the beauty of Centralized Traffic Control.

WHAT IS CTC?

A strict definition of Centralized Traffic Control, known as CTC, is a method of train control through the observance of signal indications. CTC is more than just signal hardware—it is a system of rules that govern the movement of trains. As of 1950, the Interstate Commerce Commission, a governmental regulatory agency with authority over railroad operations, defined CTC as a "a block system under which train movements are authorized by block signals whose indications supersede the superiority of trains for both opposing and following movements on the same track." In other words, traditional rules imposed by timetable and train order operation could be dispensed with by allowing trains to proceed on the authority of signal indication.

CTC signals thus perform two distinct functions; safety protection and train control. This is a direct result of blending functions of interlocking and block signal systems. CTC provides a remote operator with the ability to direct train

On the morning of September 3, 1996, a Southern Pacific westbound freight crawls through the Solitude, Utah, siding toward the west switch. The eastward home signal displays "approach" for an eastbound train, which will hold the main line during this meet between two freights on this remote desert siding east of Green River, Utah, on the former Denver & Rio Grande Western. Brian Solomon

movements over a section of railroad, similar to the way an interlocking tower operator controls the movements of trains through a local interlocking network. CTC quite literally centralizes the control of trains by giving the operator direct control of signals, which are suitably interlocked to prevent the lining of conflicting movements.

Unlike the tower operator, who traditionally would sit at a centrally located tower overlooking the railway installation he controlled, a CTC operator is often many miles from the tracks he controls. The operator of a CTC console is often a train dispatcher. Technology has allowed for the combination of traditional roles, and the dispatcher is the operator. CTC circuits replace the need for human operators at remote locations, since a dispatcher can now directly control trains without the need of middlemen. The dispatcher directs trains with electronic controls instead of using telephone or telegraph to relay train orders to remote operators (who would then copy and convey these orders to train crews) or giving instructions to tower operators along the line to tell them how to route trains and organize the movement of switches and signals.

The level of control CTC affords a dispatcher can vary greatly, depending on the type of system the railway uses. A minimal CTC installation used to govern movements on a lightly trafficked line may just give the dispatcher the control over signals, leaving train crews to line and lock the switches. In the 1940s, the Rock Island used such a system on its mainline between Omaha, Nebraska, and Limon, Colorado. A more typical CTC installation provides a dispatcher with the control of signals and motorized power switchers, as well as other apparatus in the field, such as switch heaters—which keep points free from ice and snow—while also providing him with positive indication of switch orientation and mainline track occupancy.

CTC ARRANGEMENTS

A basic CTC installation consists of a single-track mainline with passing sidings spaced at regular intervals. The spacing and length of these sidings depends on the amount of traffic a line is designed to accommodate. A lightly traveled line may have sidings of only 2,500 to 3,000 feet, located every 20 to 25 miles, while a busy single-track mainline might have sidings 9,000 feet long or longer spaced 5 to 10 miles apart.

A railroad can further increase capacity by providing long sidings with centrally located crossovers. These can be used to provide running meets—trains passing each other in opposite directions without stopping—or arranging multiple meets with two or more trains occupying sidings to meet opposing traffic.

Centrally located double crossovers provide further flexibility. A double crossover, allows trains from either track to proceed onto either track in either direction. The use of central crossovers can give a dispatcher needed flexibility if a slower train must be overtaken by a faster one and both trains also must meet oncoming traffic. This is an especially useful feature on lines that accommodate freight and passenger traffic, because passenger trains typically operate on tighter schedules and at faster speeds than freight.

In September 1942, Bessemer & Lake Erie began installing CTC between Filer (near Grove City) and Meadville Junction. Full CTC operation on the entire Bessemer mainline between XB Tower at North Bessemer and Albion, Pennsylvania, was completed on June 14, 1956. This allowed the railroad to rationalize its plant, through the removal of one mainline track and closure of traditional telegraph offices and operator stations. Bessemer's CTC was controlled from this US&S relay machine at Greenville, Pennsylvania, until 1990, when it was replaced by a modern, computer-aided system. At the time this is written, Bessemer and the Union Railroad are jointly dispatched from Duquesne. *Charles R. Tipton, Jr.; courtesy of Patrick Yough*

Another flexible single-track arrangement is the application of overlapping sidings, where the ends of sidings, one on each side of the mainline, do not connect to each other and intersect the mainline at overlapping points. This allows two trains traveling in either direction to occupy sidings while a third traverses the mainline. Alternatively, a running meet can be arranged by lining two opposing trains onto the sidings, giving them more space to complete the meet than would be possible using the sidings and mainline in the conventional manner. In effect, the sidings and mainline function as a short section of double-track.

CTC can be used to speed train movements and increase capacity. A railroad can implement a variety of improvements to facilitate these aims. A basic CTC installation will not necessarily provide track circuits on passing

sidings. If unbonded sidings are used, they will not provide positive track indications to the dispatcher. When a train enters an unbonded siding, a dispatcher will have to use a manual system for monitoring the train's location. Since track occupancy is not indicated by a track circuit, a train must receive a "restricting" aspect to enter a siding, which means the train will have to slow to a crawl to take a siding. A long train negotiating a siding at restricted speed causes delays during meets.

The simple remedy to this is track-circuited sidings that give a dispatcher positive indication of siding occupancy and allow a more favorable signal aspect at the entrance to sidings, increasing the speed at which a train can enter, traverse, and exit sidings. This expedites meets, speeds up a railroad, and increases capacity. The used of intermediate

A General Railway Signal twin-head searchlight signal at the entrance to CTC territory on the old Burlington (now Burlington Northern Santa Fe) at Aurora, Illinois. The sign on the signal informs crews that CTC rules are in effect. It is crucial that operating people know which rules apply, as this may affect how signals are interpreted. Brian Solomon

at greater speed. More advanced switch designs incorporate movable points in the frog, allowing for even faster speeds.)

Improved siding switches dramatically reduce the time needed to meet trains and facilitate rolling meets on longer sidings. This gives trains and dispatchers greater operational flexibility and increases the fluidity of a single-track line. With short trains and short sidings, the difference of 15 mph for a siding switch doesn't make a significant difference in time over the road. However, when a railroad runs long freight trains, the slower speeds required to meet trains at sidings can significantly reduce the overall capacity of a line. Today, modern American railroads routinely run freight trains at lengths of 5,000 to 10,000 feet and sometimes longer, making efficient meets an important element in contemporary traffic control. The use of 45 mph "limited" speed switches further speeds meets.

SINGLE-TRACK CTC

Some of the earliest applications of CTC were on heavily traveled single-track lines. CTC was often installed at known bottlenecks where two or more routes converged, or on steep grades. The ability for trains to proceed on signal indication greatly eased traffic flow, increasing capacity without the need to build additional tracks. In effect, CTC could be used as a fast and economical method of improving line capacity.

Many early CTC sections were short, often only a few miles long—sometimes just longer than the traditional reach of a single interlocking tower. According to *Railway Signaling*, one such early CTC single-track installation was on the Milwaukee Road between Beloit, Wisconsin, and Rockton, Illinois. Here, a 4-mile CTC section was installed in 1934 to replace a manual block staff system. The track arrangement formed a giant "X," with simple junctions at either end of the section and a grade-level crossing with Chicago & North Western near the middle of the section. At the east end of the CTC, the Milwaukee Division line from Sturtevant, Wisconsin, to Savanna, Illinois, met a branch to Janesville, Wisconsin; at the west end, a branch diverged to Rockford and Davis Junction, Illinois.

The crossing with C&NW was not originally protected by CTC but was controlled by a watchman in charge of

block signals on long sidings can allow a dispatcher to route two or more trains onto such sidings more efficiently.

The type of switch used at the ends of sidings can also speed meets. When an unbonded siding is used, a slow speed siding switch is sufficient, since a train cannot travel more than about 15 mph in any case. However, with a track-circuited siding, a medium speed switch will allow a train to enter a siding at 30 mph. (The speed at which a train can traverse a switch is regulated by the switch design. A switch with greater distance between points and frog will allow for a more gently diverging route and thus can be taken safely

gates. The dispatcher was located at Beloit and used levers to electrically control seven semaphores that directed the movements of trains over the line between the two junctions. In addition, the dispatcher could use "siding signals" to direct trains off the mainline onto passing sidings at the Beloit yard.

At the Rockton end of the CTC, a spring switch facilitated movements through the junction. This switch was normally lined for the main route to Savanna, and all trains using this route could proceed normally. Trains entering the CTC section from the branch up from Rockford could proceed safely through the trailing point spring switch, which used oil-buffer points to allow the passage of wheels against it. Only trains diverging off the mainline toward Rockford would need to manually line the switch for that route.

With the CTC, Milwaukee was able to reduce employment by eliminating the need for operators at Rockton. *Railway Signaling* noted that Milwaukee invested $15,765 for the entire installation, including grade-crossing protec-

On August 14, 1997, a westbound Conrail freight gets a "clear" aspect on the westward home signal on the main track at CP83 in Palmer, Massachusetts. In July 1986, Conrail converted the Palmer-to-Springfield section of the former Boston & Albany mainline from traditional double-track line with automatic block signals (under Rule 251) to a modern, single-track CTC system under Rule 261 with cab signals. With this new system, intermediate fixed wayside signals were removed, and fixed signals are used only at control points. By 1988, most of the B&A route from milepost 33 to Post Road had been converted. Brian Solomon

tion, and expected to save $4,255 annually through the use of CTC. This short, simple CTC section is an example of how the system was applied in the first years after its development. Railroads soon learned to take greater advantages of the potential of CTC operation on single-track and installed far larger and more complex systems.

During World War II, when traffic levels swelled quickly, rapidly outpacing American railroads' ability to handle trains efficiently, CTC was a choice solution to

123

Some railroads used a red over lunar white for a "restricting" aspect at the entrance to sidings to indicate that a train should take the siding. A "restricting" would be used on unbonded sidings. Because the signal cannot convey track occupancy, a train must proceed onto the siding at restricted speed, prepared to stop short of trains or obstructions. This photo was made on Wisconsin Central's former Soo Line mainline at Duplainville, Wisconsin, in April 1996. Brian Solomon increase single-track capacity and smooth operations. Southern Pacific implemented several short sections of CTC on its toughest single-track mountain grades, such as its Cuesta grade on the Coast Line near San Luis Obispo, California, and on its busy Tehachapi grades shared with Santa Fe, between Bakersfield and Mojave, California. Both lines suffered from steep, tortuous profiles and numerous tunnels, where double-track operation was prohibitive, and many trains required helpers.

Once a train was helped to the top of the grade, the helper engine(s) needed to return back down the grade. At times of peak traffic, the movement of light helpers could seriously impair track capacity. With the implementation of CTC, the delays stemming from helper moves was minimized. Also, dispatchers could more readily run faster trains around slow ones, maximizing the use of a single mainline.

Western Pacific was another western railroad that made good use of CTC during the war. According to S. Kip Farrington, in his book *Railroading the Modern Way*, in 1944, WP replaced traditional timetable and train order operation on 250 miles of mainline, including on its sinuous line through California's Feather River Canyon. The western-most section of its route, an 84-mile-long mainline between Oakland and Stockton, California, handled much less traffic than its mainline to the east of Stockton. Yet this line, which crests Altamont Pass at 750 feet above sea level, featured some stretches of 1 percent grade and warranted signaling improvements.

WP installed a basic CTC operation developed by Union Switch & Signal that gave the dispatcher signal controls but not switch control. Locomotive crews were responsible for lining switches manually. The system was only slightly more advanced than the APB described earlier, but WP's dispatcher could use the signals to authorize train movements. Thus WP dispatchers could direct trains to travel on the mainline between sidings as well as to take and depart sidings without the need for train orders and operators.

The basic fixed signal WP employed WP was a single-head US&S searchlight. In addition, special "siding" signals were used to direct trains off the mainline into passing sidings and out of sidings on to the mainline. These consisted of a special circular signal head below the primary searchlight that featured a black letter "S" on a white background. Distant signals (known as an approach signal on WP) were located 1.5 miles from siding switches, to warn crews of the need to stop or take sidings.

The system worked like this: if the dispatcher did not need to make a meet, the distant signal would display "clear," and the train would proceed on the mainline. If WP's dispatcher planned a meet and wanted a train to take a siding, he would light the siding signal at the end of the appropriate siding. When the train reached the distant signal, it would see "approach," giving the engineer sufficient warning to stop his train at the end of the siding.

Seeing the illuminated "S" on the take siding signal would alert the crew that it was safe to proceed onto the siding, so a brakeman would descend from the locomotive cab, reverse the siding switch (set it for the siding), and the train would line onto the siding. A brakeman riding in the caboose would manually restore the siding switch to its normal position behind the train. At the end of the siding, another signal was provided to indicate when a train could leave the siding.

As with the APB arrangement, WP provided line-side telephones at the ends of sidings, to allow crews to contact the dispatcher if necessary. In addition, the dispatcher could remotely light a lamp on the phone box to signal train crews to use the phone. Under normal circumstances, trains would have been able to meet one another strictly by following signal aspects, without needing to phone the dispatcher for instructions.

The Western Pacific mainline, like many other western mainlines, was ideally suited to CTC operation. Western Pacific installed more advanced CTC systems on other portions of its Oakland to Salt Lake City route, and by the early 1950s, the majority of its single track mainline was under the authority of CTC signaling. WP's more advanced CTC installations used conventional signals and indications to direct trains into sidings, while siding switches were operated with remote-controlled switch machines. In the West, the combination of single-track lines, great distances, heavy grades, and a predominance of freight traffic gave CTC numerous operational and cost advantages over other systems. As a result, western lines were quick to take advantage of CTC to improve their operations and to lower costs.

DOUBLE-TRACK OPERATION

Although some early examples of CTC were used on single-track lines, the system was easily adaptable for use on double-track mainlines as well. Boston & Maine was an early proponent of double-track CTC. On traditional directional double-track lines, trains can be allowed to proceed on signal indication in ABS territory using Rules 251 and 261, as described in Chapter 5. Railroads will often mix short sections of CTC with longer sections of directional double-track. CTC sections are used to control interlockings, junctions, and powered crossovers, while double-track is placed for running between controlled points.

CTC systems can be applied to as many main tracks as required by the demands of traffic. Railways may use multiple-track CTC in situations where different types of trains

At 5:50 P.M. on April 16, 1979, an SP westbound ascends the east slope of Beaumont Hill at the Mons Crossovers. Here, SP has lengthened and connected the sidings at Fingal and Mons, providing a set of double crossovers that give dispatchers flexibility in directing train movements. SP favored cantilever signal bridges, which at this location displayed green over dark for the "clear" aspect rather than the more common green over red often displayed at two-head searchlight signals. On this signal, any aspect less restrictive than red on the top head will cause the bottom head to show dark. Notice the siding signal has a third light that in this photo displays dark. This can display a lunar aspect, to allow red over red over lunar ("restricting") for a following move at restricted speed into an occupied siding. In 2002, Union Pacific reworked and resignaled this line. J. D. Schmid

are traveling at different speeds and must run around one another as per the priority of traffic.

The New York Central converted its four-track Water Level Route mainline beginning in the late 1940s. With

A Guilford Rail System locomotive gets a "medium approach" aspect on the Boston & Maine Railroad at Ayer, Massachusetts, on February 18, 2003. In 1929, B&M installed 13.5 miles of double-track CTC between Ayer and North Chelmsford on its Stony Brook Branch, controlled from the North Chelmsford tower. This system used US&S color-lights. In 1947, B&M installed a new junction at the Willows, east of Ayer, originally controlled from the Ayer tower. The more modern CTC used searchlights, which became B&M's standard signal type. Guilford's lines are now dispatched using a computer system from North Billerica, Massachusetts.
Brian Solomon

CTC, New York Central essentially reduced the number of mainlines from four to two tracks and three tracks. In most places, two main tracks with bidirectional signaling was sufficient to accommodate traffic. Sections of three tracks and controlled passing sidings were located at bottlenecks and near yards and terminals. Frequent sets of dispatcher-controlled double crossovers allowed dispatchers to route faster-moving trains around slower ones. This double-track CTC system provided sufficient flexibility for NYC to operate a full complement of freight and passenger trains.

Today, this route is among the most heavily traveled freight lines in the eastern United States. The portion east of Cleveland to the Albany, New York, area is operated by CSX, while the western portion to Chicago is run by Norfolk Southern. If you ride Amtrak between Cleveland and Chicago, you can listen to this highly efficient CTC system at work with the help of a handheld scanner. Norfolk Southern operating practice requires crews to call

out signal aspects, which tells you what is happening. As Amtrak is directed to run around freights, you will here the crew calling "approach medium" and then "medium clear" to pass through crossovers.

LATER CTC INSTALLATIONS

The advantages of CTC gave railroads a tool to economize their operations after World War II. As the New York Central example above illustrates, railroads could use CTC to reduce the number of mainline tracks needed to handle traffic. By converting a directional double-track line under Rule 251 authority to single-track CTC, a railroad could rationalize its plant and save money. Typically railroads would retain one mainline track for running while using portions of the second mainline for passing sidings.

While installing CTC, railroads often resignaled their lines at the same time. A main track would be provided with bidirectional signals, and blocks were often lengthened to reflect changes in the nature of traffic, such as the decline in passenger traffic (discussed in Chapter 1).

Another significant change with later CTC installations was the location and length of passing sidings. On traditional single-track railways, passing sidings were routinely located at or near passenger stations, where trains would make station stops and collect orders. Originally, these sidings were relatively short. By the 1950s, the greater length of freight trains required much longer sidings.

Since CTC dispensed with the need for trains to stop for train orders, locating sidings at stations had few advantages. In fact, CTC sidings are often located away from traditional stations, so they are less likely to interfere with highway grade crossings and to suffer from problems associated with built-up areas. In some situations, old station sidings were lengthened or, where stations were relatively close together, linked. Other siding location considerations include geographic situations and a line's grade profile.

CTC AT WORK

The magic of CTC is largely invisible. Unlike traditional signaling systems, where large levers and networks of rods and wires can be observed or where a train order station's telegraphers and operators could be seen performing their duties, most of a CTC system is hidden from view. Certainly the fixed signals are visible, as are the switch motors, but the mechanics of CTC are electronic, and the men and women who control the signals are usually working in an office building many miles from the tracks they control. Furthermore, many railroads employ approach-lit signals, which leave precious little for the casual observer to experience. A signal lights, a train passes, and the signal is dark again. So how does CTC work?

A train dispatcher sits at a dispatching desk. Traditionally, CTC systems were controlled using highly specialized CTC machines that consisted of rows of switches, lights, and hundreds of relays. These machines communicated with relay boxes in the field. Gradually, advances in electronics resulted in the miniaturization of control components. Today dispatchers overseeing most CTC operations from computer screens, using a keyboard and mouse to set signals and switches.

🎧 Detailed view of controls on a traditional Union Switch & Signal relay-operated CTC machine used to govern the Cotton Belt in Missouri. On top is the diagram with indicator lights to show track occupancy. Below is a row of switch-control levers, showing two positions: "normal" and "reverse." The next row is signal-control levers that have three positions: left, center, and right. At the very bottom are start buttons to initiate relay sequences. Tom Kline

In North America, the traditional CTC machine is now largely a relic, although a few of the old machines remain. They can still be found in many other countries, where traditional equipment may be preferred. The old CTC machines were built in a variety of configurations, depending on the manufacturer, scope of the CTC territory, and level of CTC control.

A typical CTC machine features a control panel with a detailed linear track diagram, representing an abstraction of the territory controlled. The diagram depicts mainlines and side tracks in schematic form; track segments are highlighted based on track circuits or sections of control. Colored lights indicate track occupancy, positions of track switches, condition of signals, and the correspondence between switch control levers and switch positions. Often a secondary diagram is mounted above the primary schematic, displaying technical information such as grade conditions, siding length and capacity, and the distances between sidings.

On January 30, 2003, eastbound Norfolk Southern train 18Q is leaving the siding at West Point, Indiana, on the old Wabash. Signal practice varied from railroad to railroad; the Wabash used a lunar-white over green "diverging clear" aspect for trains leaving sidings in CTC territory (known as Traffic Control System on Norfolk Southern). This was probably done for economic reasons, since the top head is a marker light that displays only the lunar aspect. Under NS Rule 283, "diverging clear" reads, "Proceed through turnout or turnouts at prescribed speed." NS is phasing out the lunar-white over green aspect and replacing the Wabash-era signals with modern hardware, featuring a bottom red marker below a standard Safetran (three-light) color-light signal head.
Pete Ruesch

Below the main diagram are the levers that control switches and signals in the field. These are arranged in a logical, linear fashion, corresponding to the diagram. The first row of levers below the diagram consists of a three-position variety to set signals. Signal levers were normally kept vertical. To clear a set of signals in one direction, the lever would be turned to the left; to clear them in the other direction, the lever was turned to the right.

With this lever, a dispatcher can only clear a signal, provided no conflicting routes are already lined up and track occupancy allows the clearing of signals. It should also be noted that the dispatcher does not actually select the aspect shown by the signal in the field but merely clears the

Modern dispatching uses computer screens to display track conditions and train locations. This screen shows Southern Pacific's Lafayette Subdivision controlled from Tower 86 in Houston, Texas, on September 8, 1996. White lines indicate unoccupied track. Red lines with arrows indicate trains; green arrows ahead of the red arrows show the routes lined for trains. The names of sidings are located above each siding. Train symbols are listed at the bottom of the screen. Tom Kline

signal, which will then display the most favorable aspect permitted by conditions. Since CTC signaling is a blend of interlocking and block signaling, track occupancy and interlocking conditions both affect the aspect displayed.

Directly below the signal levers are two-position levers that control switch position. Switches can be set for "normal" or "reversed"; when the lever is vertical, the switch is set "normal." Under most situations, "normal" is lined for the mainline and "reversed" for a siding or a diverging route. Directly below and vertically in line with signal and switch levers is a start button used to initiate actions.

Each set of remotely controlled switches and signals is known as a control point. A control point may be one switch at the end of a siding or a network of switches at an interlocking. Railroads use different methods for distinguishing sidings and control points. Some lines, such as Southern Pacific, give sidings traditional names that correspond directly with stations and places along the line. Looking at SP's Tehachapi crossing (now operated by Union Pacific), sidings are named Ilmon, Caliente, Bealville, Cliff, Rowan, Woodford, Walong, Marcel, and so on.

In this system, the ends of the sidings are designated by direction. So the siding at Bealville, for example, has an east and a west switch. A westbound train entering the siding, will do so by way of the east switch. Other lines, such as the former Erie Railroad, gave each end of a siding a name, again often corresponding to traditional place names. On the long siding over Attica Hill in western New York State, on the Southern Tier line (now operated by Norfolk Southern), the east switch is governed by CP Linden, located near the village of that name, while the west end of the siding is called CP Attica, located in the town center.

Another method of designating control points is simply by the milepost location. This method was popular on Conrail lines. On the Boston & Albany route, which was converted from directional double-track to a CTC single-track route with cab signals beginning in the mid-1980s, the line goes from single-track to double-track at Charlton, Massachusetts, where the control point is known simply as CP57. Charlton is at milepost 57, as measured from Boston's

South Station. This section of double-track continues down the west slope of Charlton Hill, and the next control point is located at East Brookfield, identified as CP64.

The advantage of this system is that the numerical control point designations give dispatchers a quick reference to the distances between sidings. A disadvantage is that the impersonal designations tend to make the railroad even more abstract. Instead of a railway line passing through familiar towns and places, it is just a numbered line with illuminated dots.

Back to the machine: track occupancy lights allow a dispatcher to monitor the positions of trains. Using a traditional CTC machine, a dispatcher can set up meets between trains, route trains through junctions, control crossing points, and arrange other movements, such as permitting one train to overtake another by manipulating the levers. To set up a move that lines a train into a siding, the switch lever for the siding is reversed, and the signal lever for the siding is set in the direction of the train.

So far all the levers are in position, but the move has not been executed. When the dispatcher is ready to perform the move he has set up, he presses the start buttons below the levers. The machine goes in action and initiates relay sequences. With an older machine, dispatcher hear relays working. Circuits in the machine ensure that conflicting moves cannot be arranged, and lights on the machine will indicate that the switch has reversed and signals are set. Using banks of specialized relays, the CTC machine transmits codes over the line. These codes are picked up by the appropriate field relays, which set up the circuits to move the switch points and set the signal.

Before the switches and signals can be set, the CTC machine will get information from field stations on the condition of the points and signals. This information is communicated back to the CTC machine by other codes.

The communication between the CTC control and field stations is automatic, but in practice it is comparable to the old manual block systems, where operators communicated using code to determine the condition of blocks and the like.

Most CTC installations use coded control, although this was not so with the earliest installations. The use of

On July 2, 1995, the Belt Railway of Chicago dispatcher at Clearing Yard uses a computer-aided dispatching system to govern the movement of trains over BRC's heavily traveled lines. The old General Railway Signal "Traffic Master" CTC boards are still in place beyond the computer screens to give the dispatcher a sense of the scope of his territory. Brian Solomon

coding greatly reduces the number of wires required to make CTC work. In 1977, according to Santa Fe's *Signal Training* manual, volume II, using normal direct-wire circuits, 22 wires would be required to operate a simple end-of-siding interlocking. By using a time-code system allowing for seven functions, including the switch "normal" and "reversed" controls, as many as 35 end-of-siding installations can be controlled using just two wires. With modern electronics, far more control is possible. Codes may be transmitted using a variety of systems, including line-side wires, microwave communication towers, fiber-optic cables, and directly through the rails with the most modern systems, using high-frequency track circuits.

Relay-operated CTC machines used advanced circuits to allow dispatchers to arrange a sequence of moves. Thus a train could be lined into a siding, and, once that train was in the siding and clear of the mainline, the switch could be preprogrammed to be restored to the "normal" position. This would allow trains to meet at a siding without the constant attention of the dispatcher. Today, with computer aided dispatching, far more elaborate sequences are possible.

A modern dispatching console uses computer screens in place of CTC boards to present a track diagram. This model will show track occupancy, the conditions of signals and switches, and more detailed information, such as the direction of a train. Train identification tags may indicate the train symbol, leading locomotives, and details such as the weight and length of a train, in addition to train direction. These tags follow the a train's progress across a district and make it possible to prioritize trains.

Dispatchers can line a variety of moves in advance and cancel them if conditions change. In addition, with the most advanced systems, computers can run programs that actually plan and line meets based on the speed, priority, and symbols of trains. Checks within the software prevent conflicting moves, averting the possibility that human error will cause an accident. Such automation, combined with improved communications, has made it possible for a dispatcher to control much longer and more complex territories than was possible with relay-operated CTC machines. In addition, dispatchers can use their computers to view conditions in adjacent districts, to obtain a preview of trains heading their way.

The use of radio has eased communications as well. Before radio was commonly used, dispatchers relied on trackside phones, call lights, and sometimes external trackside speakers to communicate with trains that had stopped at sidings. Often the only communication between dispatcher and locomotive engineer was the signal aspects. Today, two-way radio communication allows dispatchers to communicate directly with crews. While this is less important in CTC territory, because signals authorize movements,

it allows dispatchers to inform crews of what to expect down the line and to give them information in case of unusual circumstances. For example, if technical failure causes a switch not to reverse automatically, the dispatcher can authorize a train crew to operate the switch manually. Likewise, if a home signal fails to clear, a dispatcher can authorize a train to pass it at restricted speed.

RADIO DISPATCHING

Railways first used radio as early as the 1940s. Rock Island, Pennsylvania Railroad, and Northern Pacific were among the pioneers in the application of railroad radio. PRR's first-generation diesels were distinctive because of their large antennae used to transmit and receive radio signals. By the 1950s, the use of transistors had made radio practical for widespread railway applications. Initially, radio was used for secondary communications, to assist with switching, the yarding of trains, and the like, but not to authorize train movements.

This changed in the 1970s and 1980s, when most American railroads adopted systems for authorizing train movements by radio and abandoned traditional paper-based train order systems. The advantage of radio authorization is that it eliminates the need to have operators on the ground copy and issue written train orders to trains. Radio authorization allows a dispatcher to communicate directly with train crews and issue specific operating authority. To avoid confusion, radio authority uses standard forms and highly specific standard language. Furthermore, dispatchers must keep a careful written record of track authority, which should correspond exactly with the authority issued to trains. Similarly, when a railroad crew receives authority, it must be copied verbatim on a standard form.

Computer systems have been developed to assist dispatchers in issuing track authority, to help ensure that duplicate or overlapping authority is not issued. Verbal authority may be issued either by radio or by railroad telephone. Railroad rules require such verbal transmissions to be recorded, so that all communication between dispatcher and crews can be reviewed in case of an accident. Verbal track authority may be used to govern train movements on lines unequipped with signals and in situations where trains need dispatcher authority, such as to pass signals displaying "stop" or to move against the current of traffic.

Today, lines equipped with basic ABS signaling and APB signaling, and those that are unsignaled use verbal authority to grant trains permission to occupy track. Verbal authority is not required on lines where train movements are governed by signal indications.

Traditionally in America, track could be used in a number of ways without direct authority from a train dispatcher. Today, most American railroads have centralized the control of track usage with the dispatcher. In most situa-

Railroads began using radio in the 1940s. Today, radio is a standard tool for railroad operation. An Amtrak conductor assists in a reverse move at New Haven on November 23, 1988. Brian Solomon

tions, any use of track, be it by a train, maintenance crew, or track inspector, must be authorized by the dispatcher. A dispatcher grants authority to trains by using CTC, by issuing instructions to local operators, or by granting verbal authority. Authority to maintenance gangs and so on is usually granted by verbal authority.

Some common systems of verbal track authority used in the United States are direct traffic control, known by its initials DTC, track warrant control, known as TWC, and the Form D Control System (DCS), used under NORAC Rules. For comparison, DTC resembles the electric staff system of control, while TWC resembles train orders. Under DTC, limits are strictly defined by blocks, while TWC uses flexible limits that may be tailored to a specific train movement. A few lines, such as the South Shore and Long Island Rail Road, still use train order rules but issue train orders over the radio. Likewise, manual block systems still exist but use radio authority. The system of verbal authority rules on a line will be clearly defined by a railroad timetable.

DTC

Direct traffic control uses a system of predefined blocks, the limits of each identified by trackside signs. These state the name of the block that is beginning, the block that is ending, and the corresponding milepost location on the railroad timetable. A train is granted verbal authority to enter a block by the train dispatcher, who may issue authority to occupy a number of blocks in succession. Normally, two types of authority can be issued. Basic authority mandates the movement of a train in one direction only. "Work and Time" authority allows movement in both directions within a block, providing a specific time restriction on occupancy.

Under DTC authority as prescribed by the *General Code of Operating Rules*, the dispatcher would transmit an order to a train as follows: "Midwest Central 9994 North, with Engineer R. B. McCoy, you are authorized to proceed northward in one block, Able."

The railroad crew then repeats the order to confirm that they understand it; "Midwest Central 9994 North, with

Engineer R. B. McCoy, I am authorized to proceed north-ward in one block, Able."

Authority is not granted until the dispatcher responds to the train crew and confirms that the order has been repeated correctly. In this order, "Midwest Central 9994" refers to the locomotive in use, "North" is the direction of the train, and "Able" is the name of the block.

If more than one block is needed, the dispatcher would transmit an order this way: "Midwest Central 9994 North, with Engineer R. B. McCoy, you are authorized to proceed Northward in three blocks, Able though Charlie."

When a train clears the end its authority, it must immediately contact the dispatcher and release the block or blocks to the dispatcher. The dispatcher then repeats the release, which is confirmed by the train crew. This serves essentially the same function as releasing a manual electric staff and returning it to the machine.

TRACK WARRANT CONTROL

Track warrant control is similar to DTC, in that instructions and authority are transmitted by radio from dispatcher to train. However, TWC offers a more flexible format, using standard forms that feature a variety of potential instructions, each type of instruction having a specific line or box number. Instead of fixed blocks, a dispatcher can grant authority based on milepost or station locations. Track warrants are normally time sensitive, and each is given a unique number. A standard form may include the following lines and blanks:

Track Warrant Number:___
Issued to:____
At: ____
    2. Proceed from ____ **to** ____ **on** ____ **track.**
    3. Work between ____**and**____**on** ____ **track.**
    4. Not in effect until____
    8. Hold main track at last main point.
    10. Clear main track at last main point.
OK _____ **(time)**
Dispatcher _____
Relayed to____
Copied by____

In addition, the form may include a variety of specialized instructions, temporary speed restrictions, and other crucial information that may effect train operations. The form held by the dispatcher will match that filled in by train crews. A standard form recommended by the *General Code of Operation* rules lists 17 standard instructions. Each instruction has a box next to it. The dispatcher selects the lines of the form appropriate to the authority required and instructs a train crew to put an "X" in the relevant box for each line. Using standard lines minimizes ambiguity with the instructions.

⟲ Railroads post signs trackside to indicate the beginning and end of DTC blocks and the beginning and end of CTC territory, so that crews know where different rules for authority apply. This photo at Eagle Lake, Texas, on Southern Pacific's Sunset route (now operated by Union Pacific) shows the DTC block limit for Ramsey block and the beginning of CTC. The west-bound train in the distance will get DTC authority from the Southern Pacific dispatcher before proceeding into the Ramsey block. Tom Kline

 TRAIN CONTROL AND CAB SIGNALING

Cab signals have several benefits, including continuous signal visibility to a locomotive engineer, which greatly reduces the chance of a wayside signal being overlooked or misread. It gives the locomotive engineer peace of mind while constantly reminding him of the speed he should be traveling. In this case, a Metro-North GENESIS locomotive engineer is running on Rule 106, "Medium Cab." The cab signal indicator is the vertical white box on the beam between the windshields to the engineer's left. **Inset:** A Metro-North cab signal displays Rule 105, "Limited Cab," which indicates "proceed at limited speed" (45 mph). With M-N cab signals, engineers are not provided with route information and are expected to operate their trains in accordance with the speed dictated by cab signal aspects. In most places, the only wayside signals are at interlockings and terminals. Patrick Yough

AUTOMATIC TRAIN STOP AND TRAIN CONTROL

One of the basic failings of conventional railway signaling is the reliance on locomotive engineers to heed the warnings provided by signal aspects and to act accordingly. Despite the failsafe design of signal systems, people make mistakes, and the potential for accidents remains. Automatic train control is a backup system to protect against collision when an engineer fails to observe signals. It is designed to enforce speed control and braking restrictions and, in effect, take an element of decision making away from the locomotive engineer.

The theory behind automatic train control dates back to the 1880s, when the Pennsylvania Railroad performed the first experiments with automatic train stops. The earliest practical applications were on urban transit lines. *Railway Signal Engineer* noted in its November 1922 issue that in 1891, the Boston, Revere Beach & Lynn, a narrow-gauge suburban railway, installed an experimental, all-mechanical trip stop system. In 1899, the Boston Elevated Railway installed a more sophisticated automatic stop system, using mechanical trips that worked in conjunction with pneumatic block semaphores.

By 1908, similar systems were in service on rapid transit lines in Philadelphia and New York. In the early decades of the twentieth century, mainline steam railroads continued to experiment with automatic stop systems. In 1910, Pennsylvania Railroad introduced an electropneumatic automatic stop in conjunction with its electrified Pennsylvania Station and Hudson River tunnels in New York.

Rapid transit systems have led the way in advanced railway signaling. The reasons for this are simple—need, capability, and cost effectiveness. Rapid transit systems carry large numbers of people on short headways, often under-

ground or on elevated structures, so accidents involving rapid transit trains have the potential for large numbers of casualties. Also, because rapid transit equipment must operate in the confines of subway tunnels and other urban settings where space is at a premium, the vehicles may not be built to the same level of crashworthiness as mainline trains.

Rapid transit systems enjoy a clearly defined and comparatively small pool of equipment compared to mainline railways. Also, all equipment is normally bought, owned, and operated by one operator and is generally operated in standardized consists. Rapid transit systems are not affected by the operation of offline equipment and do not need to accommodate interchange. In general, operations are predictable and tend to follow regular patterns, making it easier to calculate maximum braking distances and other factors that affect signal placement.

For these reasons, rapid transit systems can more easily be equipped with specialized signaling equipment. It is comparatively easier to equip an entire fleet of rapid transit cars with signaling apparatus for train control and cab signals at acceptable costs. On the other hand, a mainline railway has a host of complicating factors that make the uniform application of specialized signaling difficult to implement and often prohibitively expensive.

During the World War I period, when American railroads were under control of the United States Railroad Administration, an Automatic Train Control Committee studied the application of advanced signaling, defining different types of systems and applications. In June 1922, after the USRA had relinquished control of railways, the Interstate Commerce Commission pushed forward the development of automatic train control and cab signaling with its famous order No. 13413. This order required 49 major American railroads to install automatic train controls on at least one full passenger division (locomotive and crew operating district) by February 1926. In 1924, this order was revised and expanded to include even more territory.

The effect of this mandate was the development of several practical automatic train stop and train control systems as well as cab signaling. During the 1930s and 1940s, several railroads led the way in developing and implementing advanced systems. Both Union Switch & Signal and General Railway Signal perfected commercial cab signal systems.

After World War II, a tragic accident on the Burlington near Naperville, Illinois, resulted in big changes for American railroad signaling and railroad operation. According to reports in the May and June issues of *Railway Signaling*, on April 25, 1946, Burlington's *Advance Flyer* had stopped on the mainline for an emergency equipment inspection when it was struck from behind at speed by the *Exposition Flyer*, killing 45 people. The accident occurred in multiple-track territory where all lines were protected by automatic block signaling, and the results of the subsequent investigation caused the ICC to issue new train speed restrictions in 1947.

Among the new rules was a 79 mph limit on passenger trains unless protected by a specified form of advanced signal protection: train stop, train control, or cab signal. Initially, the industry anticipated a boom in implementation of advanced signal systems. A few lines, including Union Pacific, Santa Fe, Illinois Central, Chicago & North Western, Pennsylvania, and New York Central expanded their use of advanced signaling, but the high cost of advanced signaling and the low financial return of passenger services discouraged other carriers from making the investment. Many lines responded by simply lowering speed limits to conform to the ICC's requirements for existing signaling.

The brains behind a signal system may be many miles from the hardware in the field. Banks of relays are required to make a signal system work. Some relays generate codes; others send commands to signals, switches, and other equipment in the field. Although modern signal-control equipment has been moving toward solid-state components, the proven reliability of traditional relays still makes them preferred equipment in many situations. Relays can function reliably for decades with minimal maintenance. Brian Solomon

Over the years, most of the experimental train control systems implemented in the 1920s were removed with permission of federal regulators. (The Federal Railroad Administration today oversees railroad safety.) Steam engines were known to have reached 100 mph and faster in regular daily service. But today, many lines that featured high-speed passenger services in the steam era are now limited to a 79 mph top speed. For example, on Milwaukee Road's Chicago–Milwaukee–Twin Cities line—the route of the *Hiawatha*, where until the 1947 order, trains regularly ran at speeds faster than 110 mph—Amtrak today runs no faster than the mandated 79 mph.

The reasons for the mandated speed are complex. Partly it's related to engineer reaction time, track maintenance conditions, block length, and the weight of trains.

Inside the trackside signal boxes are the relays that make the signal system work. Signal relays are rugged and are designed to last for years. Electrical components are covered in glass, to keep moisture and debris from interfering with contacts. This is a Union Switch & Signal Style-DM code transmitter relay that transmits the 75-pulse-per-minute code used to display "approach" aspects on former Pennsylvania Railroad lines. The Pennsylvania Railroad was among the first to use coded track circuits for signal aspects and cab signal. Brian Solomon

More significant, however, are two interrelated reasons: first, instead of investing in improved signal systems, most American railroads chose the short-term economic option. Second, rather than provide railroads with necessary loans, grants, subsidies, or incentives to install safety systems, the federal government mandated either implementation of expensive signal equipment or slower track speeds. At the time, the railroads were suffering from a loss of passenger traffic and were facing severe competition from growing highway and airline travel. The result is the 79 mph maximum imposed on most lines today.

TRAIN STOP AND TRAIN CONTROL AT WORK

Train control systems are either intermittent or continuous types. The earliest form of intermittent train stop was applied on rapid transit lines, using a mechanical arm that is raised at a signal displaying a "stop" aspect. If a train runs past a "stop" aspect, the arm triggers the air brake line, making an "emergency" brake application.

This type of system is ill-suited to heavy rail operations. Instead, of a mechanical system, an inductive train stop was devised. Intermittent inductive train stop systems use fixed induction coils, called transponders, placed trackside at strategic locations, usually in conjunction with automatic block signals. An induction receiver on the locomotive senses data from the transponder corresponding to the displayed signal aspects.

Induction systems follow failsafe principles. With a basic system, if a signal displays "clear," no warning is needed, but if any "restrictive" aspect is passed, a warning is sounded. The engineer must act on the warning immedi-

ately, or the brakes are automatically applied to stop the train. Usually, once brakes are applied automatically, they cannot be normally released, so the engineer must get out of his seat to reset a switch. A variety of transponders has been developed.

Both intermittent and continuous train control systems use fixed blocks in the same way an automatic block system does. Instead of wayside transponders, continuous train control systems send information through track circuits, using high-frequency alternating current at a low voltage to transmit pulse codes. Code rates are described in electrical pulses per minute, typically 75, 120, and 180 pulses. Each code indicates specific track conditions that corresponds to wayside signal aspects. Coded data is picked up by induction receivers on the locomotive, where it is amplified and decoded.

With a typical four-block train control system, four codes are used. The code signal carrier frequency is 100 Hz (alternating current) to distinguish it from commercial 25 Hz and 60 Hz electric power. Field relay stations produce and transmit the code signals.

Various types of relays have been developed as pulse-code generators. Today, some modern systems use solid-state code generators, although relays are often favored because of their durability. For basic aspects, commonly 180 code is used for "clear," 120 code for "approach medium," 75 code for "approach," and no code for "restricting." If train control equipment fails on the ground or on the train and the code is interrupted, the most restrictive signal code—no code—is received, insuring failsafe operation.

The system works like this: when a signal displays "clear," the 180 code rate is transmitted through the rail ahead of the signal, so that a train running on the track receives the "clear" aspect. If the next signal displays "advance approach," when the train enters that block it will pick up the 120 code rate, and the train control system will give the locomotive engineer an audible warning, which must be acknowledged. With each change in the code rate, the engineer receives a warning. Some train control systems provide only a warning and rely on the locomotive engineer to take action. Others automatically apply the brakes if train speed is not reduced within a specified period after the warning.

The introduction of coded systems has had various benefits, including greater reliability and reduction of line wires needed for multi-aspect signaling. Coded control can also be applied to wayside hardware and onboard equipment. This has been especially advantageous for the development of more sophisticated block systems.

CAB SIGNALS

Taking train control one step further, a visual display of track conditions is placed in the locomotive cab, re-creating the aspect displayed by the last wayside signal. Since cab signal information is obtained in the same way as train stop and train control, both intermittent and continuous cab signal systems are available, and they may be used in conjunction with other signal systems. In some situations, cab signals are used with train control but without fixed signals between interlocking control points, offering further cost savings.

Santa Fe operated passenger trains at a top speed of 90 mph and equipped high-speed lines with intermittent automatic train stop, using fixed-induction transponders. One of these transponders is seen at Model, Colorado, at the bottom left of the photo. The semaphores are Union Switch & Signal Style T-2. These were of a three-position upper-quadrant type that used a top-of-mast mechanism. Typical semaphore height was 22 feet, 6 inches from ground to mechanism. Tom Kline

Two-aspect and four-aspect continuous systems are among the most common in the U.S. In a two-aspect system, cab signals display either "clear" or "restricting." Chicago & North Western used this system with train control and without wayside intermediate signals on its Chicago-Omaha mainline, west of Chicago suburban territory (now the UP) Between control points, trains were governed strictly by cab signal. The two-aspects allow trains to proceed at either "normal" speed or at "restricted" speed, depending on conditions ahead.

A drawback to two-aspect cab signaling is that it tends to impede track capacity by spacing trains relatively far apart and can compound congestion when several trains are traveling in the same direction toward a junction or terminal. Trains traveling closely together will run on restricted speed, which is much slower than normal track speed.

Introducing more aspects increases the flexibility of a cab signal system and line capacity. A four-aspect system, such as that now used by Metro-North on former New Haven and New York Central lines in suburban New York, allows trains to safely operate on closer headways than was possible with either fixed wayside signals or two- or three-aspect cab signal systems.

To understand this, it is important to review basic block system principles: the closer blocks are spaced, the more trains can operate over the line. The length of blocks is dictated by braking distance. If block length is less than needed to stop a train, the signal system must provide advance information on the condition of blocks ahead. This is the premise for three-block, four-aspect signaling described in Chapter 5.

With four-aspect wayside signaling, a train following another may repeatedly received either "approach-medium" or "approach" aspects. When this happens, the following train is slowed to less than normal speed. However, if the train ahead accelerates or switches to a diverging route and is out of the path of the following train, the following train will be able to resume full speed only when the engineer sees the next wayside signal.

Four-aspect cab signaling affords greater capacity, because the signal in the cab reflects the condition of the last signal passed. As soon as the signal is upgraded, the engineer can respond. With short, relatively fast trains, such as those operated in congested commuter territory, the ability to speed up immediately, without needing to travel the length of a block to receive an improved signal, allows trains to follow more closely. This increases capacity and helps keep a line fluid.

Cab signaled territory has changed the way engineers run trains. With wayside signals, engineers anticipate the condition of the next signal. If they passed an "approach" signal, they need to slow their train in preparation to stop short of the next signal. With cab signaling, signal aspects are assigned speed indications. On Metro-North, according to their Rule 104, these are "Normal Cab," which indicates normal track speed; "Limited Cab," which indicates travel at limited speed (typically 45 mph for passenger trains); "Medium Cab," which indicates medium speed (30 mph for passenger trains); and "Restricted Cab," which indicates restricted speed (less than 15 mph and prepared to stop short of trains, obstructions, etc.)

The condition of the next signal shouldn't matter, nor should diverging routes. In theory, with cab signals an engineer should be able to operate strictly according to the speed dictated by signal

Chicago & North Western used a two-aspect continuous inductive cab signal with automatic train control on its Chicago-to-Omaha mainline. This cab signal displays a "restricting" aspect, which mimics the same aspect displayed by a color-light signal. When "restricting" is displayed, a warning signal sounds at a regular interval that the engineer must acknowledge, or the brakes will set automatically. Brian Solomon

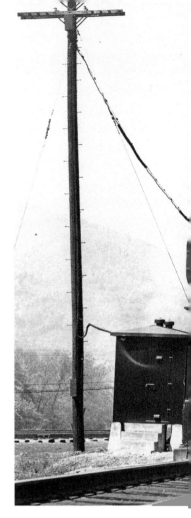

The cab signal receiver is placed ahead of the leading wheels of a locomotive or self-propelled railcar. Here, on a former New Haven Railroad FL9, the receiver can be seen just above the rail, below the locomotive plow and ahead of the brake equipment for the leading truck. Patrick Yough

Chesapeake & Ohio's "JD" Tower at the east end of Clifton Forge controlled movements between the James River Subdivision (*left*) and the Mountain Subdivision (*right*). Note the sign to the right of the signals that reads "End of Train Control," informing engineers of the change in signaling at this location. C&O preferred Union Switch & Signal color-lights on new installations from the 1920s onward. According to *Railway Signaling,* this layout was rebuilt in 1927. The photo was made on May 11, 1947. Bruce Fales; Jay Williams collection

indication. In actual operation, many factors come into play that affect how an engineer handles a train, so route knowledge as well as understanding of operating patterns may allow for smoother operation. However, safety cannot be compromised, because automatic train control prevents an engineer from disregarding cab signal warnings.

HIGH-SPEED CAB SIGNALING

Amtrak now operates its *Acela Express* trains at speeds up to 150 mph between Boston and New Haven. Since these fast electric trains share the line with much slower traffic, an advanced cab signal and train control system was developed called Advanced Civil Speed Enforcement System (ACSES). This provides nine aspects for high-speed operation while allowing trains equipped with the older four-aspect cab signal equipment to continue to operate (at less than maximum speed). New aspects are used for faster track speeds and to allow trains equipped with ACSES to move through new high-speed crossovers at speeds as fast as 80 mph.

As with other cab signal systems, each aspect change is accompanied by an audible warning. In addition to basic cab signal aspects, modern trackside transponders warn of both permanent and temporary speed restrictions along the line. This is different from conventional signal systems, which rely on a locomotive engineer's route knowledge to negotiate speed restrictions. In addition, transponders enforce "positive stops" (absolute stops) at interlockings, so that high speed trains cannot overshoot "stop" signals and cross the route of another train. The ACSES cab signal is a modern, sophisticated train control system designed to ensure safe operation for America's fastest trains. It is comparable to systems used by the French TGV, German ICE, and Japanese Shinkansen high-speed trains.

POSITIVE TRAIN CONTROL

The future of railway signaling may lie in new technology now being developed and tested. Positive Train Control (sometimes called Precision Train Control) blends several new technologies to protect trains and highway crossings. Unlike most traditional systems, it does not rely on track circuits and fixed blocks for train control. Instead, PTC incorporates satellite-based global positioning technology, with computer-aided speed and distant measuring systems and trackside transponders to locate trains and keep them operating at safe intervals. This system uses floating blocks that move with the train. In addition, grade-crossing protection is controlled by radio transmissions from the trains.

PTC has a variety of potential applications. It may be used to allow high-speed passenger trains to operate on the same tracks as normal-speed freight traffic, fulfilling federal safety requirements for services operating faster than 79 mph without the need for elaborate ground-based automatic train control systems. Someday, PTC systems may replace traditional signal technology and hardware. Unlike traditional signaling systems, PTC uses relatively little ground-based hardware, so it requires less maintenance and is less subject to weather-related failures, vandalism, and mechanical component failure. As this is being written in 2003, the former Alton route from Chicago to St. Louis was being equipped with a PTC prototype system, to allow Amtrak trains to travel at speeds up 110 mph.

GRADE-CROSSING SIGNALS

In America, modern railroad/high-way grade-crossing protection typically consists of flashing lights, automatic gates, and a ringing bell. Warning is provided to motorists to stop at railroad crossings, but since crossings are not interlocked with block signals and trains are often incapable of stopping, the burden of responsibility is on the motorist. Brian Solomon

RAILWAY/HIGHWAY CROSSINGS at grade

pose a special difficulty for railway signaling. Closely regulated railway traffic must avoid contact with loosely regulated highway traffic. American railways have a great many grade crossings with highways, and trains cross highways tens of thousands of time every day. Unfortunately, highway crossings remain today one of most likely locations for railway accidents in the United States.

The best solution to avoid the potential of crossing collisions is by the grade separation of railways and highways. Highway underpasses and overbridges can safely separate road and railway traffic, but this is the most expensive solution. Estimates vary, but grade separation can cost twenty times more than basic grade-crossing protection. For this reason, grade separation is often deemed impractical.

In other countries with intensive railway networks, such as the United Kingdom, France, and Germany, grade crossings are relatively rare. British railways were built to high standards from the beginning. By the nature of the way the lines were laid out in the U.K. and laws regarding fencing of railways, railway lines tended to avoid grade-level road crossings.

European mainlines tend to operate fast trains on frequent intervals, so numerous grade crossings would pose both a significant inconvenience and a hazard to motorists and trains. Therefore, in Western Europe, railways are viewed as an essential part of a nation's public infrastructure, and taxpayers readily accommodate the cost of improvements, such as grade separation.

Basic grade-crossing protection consists of just a set of crossbucks with a verbal warning to motorists. The crossbucks symbolized a set of crossbones, a traditional symbol of danger. Today, crossbucks often read just "Railroad Crossing," but earlier signals, such as this one, photographed along the Santa Fe at Dillwyn, Kansas, included the admonishment "Look Out for the Cars." Tom Kline

AMERICAN GRADE CROSSINGS

In the United States prior to the 1920s, railway grade-crossing protection was not standardized, and many types of protection were used to warn road traffic (which until about 1914 was primarily horsedrawn) of approaching trains. Lightly traveled crossings were guarded by simple warning signs, while busier crossings were protected by flag-wielding watchmen who would stop traffic when trains approached.

As early as the 1880s, automatic gates were suggested to block railway crossings when trains approached. Hall disc signals were among the types of early automatic signaling used to warn drivers. The first flashing light signal wasn't introduced until 1911—when, according to Brignano and McCullough's *Search for Safety*, a signal patented by L. S. Brach was installed on the Jersey Central at Sewaren, New Jersey. This odd signal used a circular pattern of lights to warn road traffic.

During the 1910s and 1920s, railway organizations coordinated efforts to establish nationwide standards for grade-crossing protection. The X-shaped grade-crossing sign, commonly known as a "crossbuck," has been used since the late 19th century. Brignano and McCullough suggest that the crossbuck emulated crossbones, a universal symbol of danger. Various written warnings have been used on crossbucks, including admonishing slogans such as "Watch Out for the Cars." Today, the standard crossbuck displays the words "Railroad Crossing." The angle of the "X" has evolved, too. Older crossbucks used a broader "X" arrangement with unequal angles. Modern signs use an "X" crossing with right angles.

Today, lightly used grade crossings may feature only a basic crossbuck, sometimes with a black sign below that reads "Stop, Look, and Listen." At such locations, the burden of safe crossing is on the attentive motorist. Approaching trains are normally required to blast the horn in a standard pattern of whistles: two successive long blasts, followed by a short blast and a third long blast. Although a train whistling at a grade crossing has been generally accepted as a safe practice for warning highway traffic, in

For many years, the wigwag was standard grade-crossing protection in the West. A wigwag protects Southern Pacific's Siskiyou Line at Ray Gold, Oregon, in May 1990. Notice the Union Switch & Signal Style-B semaphores in the distance. Brian Soloman **Right:** The Magnetic Signal Company of Los Angeles was a large supplier of wigwag grade-crossing protection. Brian Solomon

some localities it has been banned because the sound disturbs local residents. In these situations, the motorist must be especially vigilant when crossing, as an engineer will sound the horn only in emergency situations.

One of the first standard types of automated visual grade-crossing warning was the automatic flagman, a signal commonly known as a "wigwag." According to Santa Fe documents, the wigwag was adopted as a standard crossing device by the American Railway Association in 1923. A standard wigwag is actuated by a track circuit and consists of a paddle with a red lamp that gracefully swings back and forth in a horizontal pattern when a train approaches. A wigwag is usually accompanied by a bell.

Stationary, electrically actuated bells have long been

used to warn of approaching trains and are now a standard audible warning device. Among the most common types of wigwag signals are those manufactured by the Magnetic Signal Company of Los Angeles. For many years, the wigwag was the preferred type of grade-crossing protection in the Midwest and Far West. They have been largely supplanted by modern flashing signals and crossing gates, but as of this writing, a few wigwags are still in service in the U.S.

Another early standard automatic grade-crossing warning was a signal that featured a revolving stop sign in a metal frame. Normally, when the railway was clear, the stop sign would face away from the highway, but when a train approached, the stop sign would snap into place facing the direction of highway traffic. Such a signal is likely to capture the attention of motorists, who are attuned to pause at stop signs.

The flaw with this type of protection is that a typical octagonal stop sign is normally obeyed as a "stop and proceed" signal by highway traffic rather than as a "stop and stay" signal, which is required of a railway grade-crossing signal. Like the wigwag, this type of grade-crossing protec-

A time exposure of a Union Pacific train rolling through a crossing west of Friesland, Wisconsin, demonstrates a wigwag in action. A few of these old signals remain, despite the predominance of grade-crossing flashers and automatic gates. John Leopard

tion has been largely phased out, despite its one-time widespread application, especially in the Upper Midwest. The Griswold Signal Company of Minneapolis was a primary supplier of these signals, commonly known as "Griswolds" among railroaders.

Today, the standard form of automated grade-crossing protection in the United States is a signal consisting of a pair of flashing red lights mounted on a post with crossbucks, which may be accompanied by a warning bell. This signal may also include a sign displaying the number of tracks protected. Although now the most recognizable of all American railroad signals, it is important to recall that it has become a standard only since the 1920s.

At busy crossings or in situations where additional protection is required, a flashing-light crossing is often combined with an automatic gate that lowers across a roadway after the lights begin to flash. According to GRS's *Elements of Railway Signaling*, a typical flashing-light signal is mounted on an aluminum pole 4 inches in diameter that

stands 13 feet tall. It is normally located at least 15 feet from the nearest active rail and 6 feet from the side of the roadway. The lamps used by the typical flashing light signal are in the 15 to 25 watt range and are designed to flash between 35 and 55 times per minute. The flashing alternates from one lamp to the other in a constant, recognizable pattern that should immediately identify the grade-crossing signal in all weather.

The lens of the red light is designed to provide an even light both horizontally and vertically and to focus light toward the direction of highway traffic. The signals are oriented to be adequately visibly on a tangent road 1,500 feet before the grade crossing. A small sighting hole in the lamp housing faces toward the railway, so that a locomotive engineer can see if the signals are functioning properly when approaching a crossing.

In situations where a single mast may not provide enough protection, such as on a multilane highway, where greater sighting distance may be needed, or where the significance of the railway crossing needs to be impressed upon motorists, a cantilever gantry may be erected over a highway. On a four-lane highway, such a gantry may hold several sets of flashing lights. At complex highway/railway junctions, it is often necessary to aim sets of flashing lights at several angles, to ensure that motorists see the signals, regardless of their direction of approach to the crossing.

On lines using more than one track, it is standard procedure to place a sign on the crossing signal that indi-

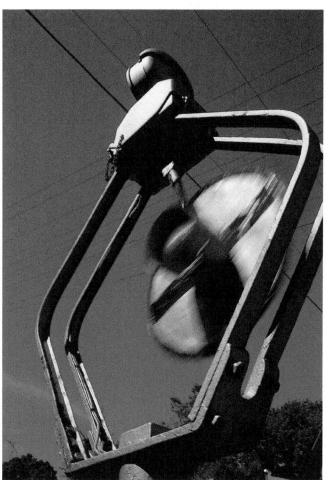

⮑ One style of wigwag popular on lines in the Midwest used a full supporting frame rather than a cantilever arm to support the automatic flag. This signal has been activated by an approaching train. As the arm swings back and forth, it rings the bell on top of the signal. This slowly swinging arm is designed to attract motorists' attention. Brian Solomon

🔊 Another wigwag was the three-position variety. When the signal was not activated, the flag would remain tucked under the black housing. When activated, the flag would be released and would swing back and forth. Brian Solomon

cates the number of tracks. This is especially important on multiple-track (two or more) mainlines, where several trains may occupy the crossing simultaneously. Multiple-track lines can pose especially dangerous situations. An impatient motorist, having been blocked by a train, may be ready to charge across a multiple-track crossing as soon as one train has cleared and may proceed before checking to see if a second train is bearing down on the crossing from the opposite direction. Many serious accidents are caused when a car is struck by the second train on a crossing. The hazards of double-track railways seem to elude modern motorists, and multiple-track operations appear to be entirely beyond their contemplation.

On multiple-track lines, automatic gates are often installed, even when the crossings are only lightly used. In the U.S., typical crossing gates offer only a psychological barrier to discourage motorists from proceeding over a crossing. These barriers block only half the roadway and are made of easily breakable wood or fiberglass, so that they

149

The Griswold Signal Company of Minneapolis manufactured revolving-stop-sign grade-crossing signals. For many years, revolving-stop-sign signals were preferred in Minnesota and were used throughout the upper Midwest. When the highway crossing was open to traffic, the stop sign was parallel to the road, so that it was not visible to traffic. The sign was counterweighted, so that when a train shunted the track circuit, an electric latch released, and the sign quickly turned by gravity to face the road. This was often accompanied by flashing lights. When the train left the track circuit, a 12-volt direct-current motor turned the stop sign back to the parallel position. Brian Solomon

🎧 GE-built U30Cs lead a Delaware & Hudson freight toward a grade crossing at Delanson, New York. The crossing is protected by traditional grade-crossing flashers and crossbucks. For many years, railroads painted grade-crossing signal masts black and white, while block signal and interlocking signal masts were painted black, as shown here. Today, masts are normally painted silver, to make them more visible. Note the cast-iron crossbucks and button reflectors on subsidiary lettering. Jim Shaughnessy

cannot trap a vehicle on a crossing. The protection offered by grade-crossing gates works only if the barriers are obeyed. When a crossing appears clear, it is easy enough to drive around lowered barriers—a dangerous and often fatal mistake made by suicidal motorists, unwilling to wait a few minutes while a train passes.

HOW AUTOMATIC CROSSING SIGNALS WORK

Grade-crossing signals can be actuated by a variety of track circuits. A traditional direct-current, battery-powered relay circuit has often been used for grade-crossing signals. On a typical bidirectional, single-track railway, three circuits are needed—one on either side of the grade crossing and a central circuit located at the crossing. The approach circuits use stick relay circuits (similar to those used in APB signaling; see Chapter 5) to detect the direction of travel. When the approach circuit detects the presence of a train, it actuates circuits that cause the grade-crossing signals to begin flashing.

Many rural crossings are protected by crossbucks and flashing lights. When the crossing is activated, motorists are expected to heed the warning. Unfortunately, some choose to ignore the lights. Double-track lines are especially dangerous, because an inattentive motorist may spot a slow-moving train on one track, make the ill-advised decision to cross without looking in the other direction, and drive into the path of a fast-moving train on the other track. In Autumn 1964, a Reading Ramble steam excursion approaches a crossing in eastern Pennsylvania. Richard Jay Solomon

With a basic circuit, the signals will continue to flash until the rear end of the train clears the central circuit at the crossing, at which time the signals return to their inactive state. Directional signal circuits are necessary, so that trains do not reactivate grade-crossing signals when passing the approach circuit on the far side of the crossing. Also, without directional circuiting, grade-crossing signals would continue to operate after a train has passed.

More modern grade-crossing circuits use frequency-shift overlay circuitry (also called audio frequency overlay) transmitted through the rails. According to GRS, these high-frequency circuits use sophisticated electronic transmitters and receivers operating on distinct channels between 618 and 20,900 Hz. They do not require insulated rail joints, as do basic direct-current circuits, and need only two track circuits to activate crossing signals.

A transmitter uses an electronic oscillator to generate a carrier signal, which is then modulated for control purposes and sent through a signal amplifier and coupling unit for transmission through the rails. A receiver uses similar equipment, including a signal detector to receive the high-frequency signals and interpret their meanings. Frequency-shift overlay circuits can be used over a distance of several miles, much longer than conventional direct-current battery circuits, and circuits at difference frequencies can be overlapped without risk of interference. By using two overlapping circuits, three track-occupancy sections can be arranged.

Among the difficulties in designing grade-crossing circuits is adjusting the timing to make the crossing signals operate in a timely fashion. Signal lights must illuminate soon enough to allow motorists to stop safely when circuits indicate an approaching train. Thus the design of a circuit must take into consideration the speed of both highway traffic and trains. Since motorists are notoriously impatient, circuits must be designed so that traffic delays are kept to a minimum before a train occupies the crossing. If motorists are delayed too long, they may be tempted to drive through the crossing.

In situations where all trains travel at roughly the same speed, the design of a crossing circuit is fairly straightforward. Difficulties arise when trains traveling at greatly varied speeds use a crossing or when trains must routinely stop short of crossings after entering the approach circuit. The latter situation poses problems where passenger stations, passing sidings, or freight yards are located near highway crossings. With basic circuitry, a train may activate grade-crossing signals for a prolonged period before it passes through the crossing. This may result from being stopped at a station or for other reasons and leaves the crossing signals active without a train in sight. If this sort of activity occurs routinely, it creates a dangerous situation by encouraging ambivalence in motorists, who may incorrectly assume the signals are broken.

To provide better grade-crossing protection, modern grade-crossing signals may incorporate a variety of motion detectors and motion predicting computers, in addition to

This tunable joint coupler allows variable continuity in the track circuit around an insulated rail joint. Used in conjunction with high-frequency track circuits, it provides low impedance to the frequency needed to pass the joint and high impedance to all track-circuit frequencies. It can be used where a succession of highway crossings needs overlapping approach circuits. This tunable joint coupler is marked by a "shunt" plate on the ties. Tom Kline

and in coordination with sophisticated track circuits. These devices enable activation of grade-crossing signals to more closely reflect the actual approach time of trains. It also makes them less likely to remain active when trains have stopped or are approaching a crossing at slow speed from a far distance. Devices can be designed so that when sensors detect motion, they will automatically de-energize (or shunt) track circuits and activate grade-crossing circuits. However, if motion ceases for a period of time, these devices will then restore the track circuit to its normal, unshunted state, shutting the signals off.

A motion sensor is often used in combination with timed relays, so that minor electrical interruptions or brief train stops do not cause signals to go on and off several times in a short period. The use of sophisticated motion sensors is aided by frequency-shift overlay circuitry. For example, one type of motion sensor transmits a signal through the rail to detect motion when an approaching train shorts the circuit. The faster a train approaches, the

This experimental four-quadrant crossing near Madison, Wisconsin, on Wisconsin & Southern features gates that lock in place. Such protection has the advantage of preventing highway traffic from crossing when a train is approaching. With the more common variety of automatic gates, traffic has the option of going around. Brian Solomon

more quickly the device will sense the train. It is designed so that a slow-moving train will activate the sensor only when the train is relatively close.

In situations where trains may approach crossings at a wide range of speeds, it may be desirable for railroads to use computers to calculate the speed of the train and actuate crossing signals at the appropriate intervals. In this way, signals will give a constant warning interval to motorists, regardless of the speed of the train.

In North American practice, grade-crossing signals are not normally integrated with block or interlocking signals. In the vast majority of situations, signals governing train movements operate entirely independently of grade-crossing signals. When a train receives a "clear" signal to proceed, this signal is given without consideration to condition of grade crossings. The speed and enormous mass of trains, especially long, fast freights, often makes it impractical for trains to stop short of grade crossings. For this reason, adequate grade-crossing signals must be provided for highway traffic.

In other countries, the situation is different. For example, in Britain and Ireland, gates that block the road completely provide absolute protection, preventing highway traffic from crossing tracks via either lane as a train approaches. In these situations, the grade crossing is observed either by a locally positioned gatekeeper who is in charge of operating the gates or remotely, by way of closed-circuit television cameras. Block signals are interlocked with grade-crossing signals, so that trains cannot receive a "clear" signal until full highway protection is in place.

With older crossing systems, gates often swing normally open to the road and closed across the railway tracks themselves. A distant signal warns trains of the position of the gates, so that an engineer will have ample time to slow and stop a train if it arrives before the gates are opened. Normally, gatekeepers are alerted to the approach of trains by railway employees down the line so that gates can be closed against the highway in advance of train movements. The advantages to this system are obvious: it is almost impossible for a grade-crossing collision to occur. Impatience on the part of the motorist cannot result in their foolish jumping of a crossing, and trains cannot cross a highway until a railway employee deems it safe to do so. In situations where interlocking signals are located near crossings, the crossing gates must be closed and locked against the highway before the railway signals can be cleared.

While this system is much safer, it is far more costly to maintain, as railway employees must be stationed either at gates or at a central office. Thus the cost of operating an individual crossing is much higher than simply maintaining an automatic flashing light and bell actuated by a track circuit. Another drawback is that crossings may be blocked against the road for several minutes ahead of a train, potentially causing a greater delay to highway traffic than automatic crossings.

In the United States, where there are tens of thousands of crossings, such costs have been deemed prohibitive and the operations impractical. In many areas, railway lines may see only one or two trains a day, and numerous highway crossings are lightly traveled. Since American trains are much longer and heavier than those in Britain, it would be far more complex to integrate grade-crossing signals with railway automatic block signals.

These sorts of situations demonstrate that the cost of signaling is often as important a consideration as total safety. Although grade crossings can be made safer, often it is deemed too expensive to do so. It is cheaper and perhaps more practical to place the burden of responsibility on highway users and afford them the freedom of decision rather than provide absolute protection.

With this in mind, American locomotives are fitted with a variety of safety warning devices, including bright

An interesting combination of a wigwag, crossbucks, and automatic gates is used at this bilingual railway grade crossing on the Canadian National, near St. Lambert, Quebec. On November 27, 1957, a Canadian National Railway 4-8-4 leads a long freight. Even if crossing protection didn't arrest a motorist's attention, one would hope the sight of this stunning locomotive hard at work would! Jim Shaughnessy

headlights, flashing "ditch lights," loud multitone horns, and bells, to warn motorists and people on or near the railway right-of-way of an approaching train. Locomotives are designed to withstand crashes with highway vehicles, and since the late 1980s, locomotives have been made more crashworthy with the introduction of the North America Safety Cab. Armored locomotives are designed to protect railroad crews in the event of a collision. In a grade-crossing crash, the size and mass of a train give it an enormous advantage over a highway vehicle.

GLOSSARY

Absolute Permissive Block (APB): A system of automatic block signaling that uses permissive signals for following moves but absolute signals for opposing moves, which facilitates the flow of traffic without compromising safety. See Chapter 5.

Absolute signal: A fixed signal that must not be passed when displaying a "stop" aspect. A home signal is often also an absolute signal.

Approach aspect: A cautionary aspect often used to slow trains that are approaching a home signal displaying a "stop" aspect. In most modern rulebooks, this signal is indicated with a signal yellow light or a semaphore in a 45-degree diagonal position.

Approach signal: *See* **Distant signal**

Aspect: The information displayed by a fixed signal. An aspect conveys an indication that has a specific meaning in accordance with a railway's rules.

Automatic block signal: A block signal that is part of an automatic block system, actuated by a track circuit and designed to reflect track condition and block occupancy. It may be combined with an interlocking network.

Automatic block signal system: A network of defined blocks controlled by a track circuit and governed by automatic block signals and/or cab signals.

Block: A length of track between clearly defined limits, used to separate trains. Occupancy may be governed by fixed signals of either manual or automatic varieties, cab signal, staff, token, or written or verbal orders, as prescribed by the rules of the railway operating the line.

Block instrument: A telegraphic instrument used to communicate the condition of a block.

Block signal: A fixed signal for trains governing the entrance to a block.

Block system: A network of consecutive blocks used to separate trains by distance.

Cab signal: A signal system that displays signal aspects in the cab of a locomotive. It may be used in conjunction with fixed wayside signals or may be independent of them. It may also be combined with automatic train control. See Chapter 8.

Centralized Traffic Control (CTC): An interlocked remote control system that allows an operator/dispatcher to direct train movements over a railway line by signal indication. Typically, it gives the operator control of switches, signals, and other operating devices. Originally, "cTc" was a trade name of the General Railway Signal Company but "CTC" is now applied to most such systems, regardless of manufacturer. See Chapter 6.

Color-light signal: Signal hardware that uses colored lights to display aspects.

Color-position-light: Signal hardware that displays signal aspects through both the color and position of lights. Basic aspects are modified for speed signaling with colored marker lights.

Direct Traffic Control (DTC): A system used for dispatching trains by radio that uses fixed blocks.

Distant signal: A signal used preceding a home signal to give advance warning of the condition of that signal. Sometimes called an "approach" signal.

Fishtail: A style of semaphore blade consisting of an inverted chevron that resembles a fish tail. Often used for distant signals.

Fixed signal: A signal at a fixed location used to govern train movements.

Following movement: A train following another over the same section of track in the same direction. The opposite of an opposing movement.

Frog: The part of a switch or crossing that permits wheel flanges to cross rails at an angle.

Home signal: A fixed signal governing the entrance to a block, interlocking plant, or controlled point. In many situations, it is an absolute signal under control of a tower or dispatcher and thus must not be passed when displaying a "stop" indication. It is typically preceded by a distant signal.

Indication: The information given by a signal aspect.

Industrial track: A side track used for switching or car storage that is not used for normal running and may be not under control of a block system. Typically, movement on such tracks must be made a restricted speed.

Interlocking plant: A network of switches, signals, and locks mechanically or electrically interconnected, to ensure a predetermined order that prevents the arrangement of conflicting and opposing movements through the plant.

Interlocking signal: A signal controlled through mechanical or electrical means and interconnected with related switches and signals to prevent the arrangement of conflicting and opposing movements through an interlocking plant. Normally, such signals are absolute and thus cannot be passed when displaying a "stop" indication.

Junction: A place where tracks come together. Typically used to describe the merging or crossing of two or more routes.

Limited speed: Typically not faster than 45 mph.

Lower-quadrant semaphore: A semaphore that displays aspects in the lower quadrant.

Mainline: A primary artery of a railroad, which may consist of one or more main tracks.

Main: A track designated for running.

Medium speed: Typically not faster than 30 mph.

NORAC: Northeast Operation Rules Advisory Committee. A set of modern railroad operating rules that has been adopted by many railroads and commuter rail agencies operating in the Northeastern United States.

Normal speed: The maximum speed authorized on a line. This may vary by train type. Some railroads will post limits indicating the maximum speed at which each type of train may travel.

Opposing movement: The movement of a train made in the direction opposite direction to another train. The opposite of a following movement.

Permissive aspect: An aspect displayed by a manual block signal that permits movement at restricted speed into an occupied block.

Permissive signal: A fixed signal, usually in automatic block territory, that displays "stop and proceed" or, in some situations, "restricting" as its most restrictive aspects. Such signals are clearly distinguished from absolute signals by markings such as a number plate or letter markings.

Points: The movable part of a switch, used to direct wheel flanges from one set of tracks to another. In the British lexicon, the term "points" is used to describe the whole switch.

Position-light: A signal that gives aspects using rows of lights to mimic aspects of upper-quadrant semaphores.

Restricting aspect: A signal aspect that authorizes a train to travel at restricted speed.

Restricted speed: A slow speed defined by railroad rules. The actual speed varies among different rulebooks. NORAC defines movement at restricted speed under Rule 80, which states,

Movement at Restricted Speed must apply the following three requirements as the method of operation:

1) Control the movement to permit stopping within one half the range of vision short of;

a) Other trains or railroad equipment occupying or fouling the track,

b) Obstructions,

c) Switches not properly lined for movement,

d) Derails set in the derailing position,

e) Any signal requiring a stop.

AND

2) Look out for broken or mis-aligned track.

AND

3) Do not exceed 20 mph outside interlocking limits and 15 mph within interlocking limits. This restriction applies to the entire movement, unless otherwise specified in the rule or instruction that requires Restricted Speed.

Rulebook: A detailed list of rules that define the method of conduct regarding railway operations for the use of railway employees.

Semaphore: A traditional signal that displays aspects by the position of its arm, or blade. It may be operated by manual, mechanical, pneumatic, or electrical means and may be used in combination with colored lights.

Searchlight signal: A variety of color-light that uses a single lamp and a focused beam. Sometimes called a "target signal" because of its shape.

Siding: A running track used for the meeting or passing of trains.

Signal: In this book, a signal generally refers to fixed signal hardware, as opposed to a sign made by an employee. In the strictest definition, a signal can be interpreted as sounds, lights, symbols, semaphores, or signs that are used to direct, govern, or control railway operations. Railway rules often do not distinguish between a fixed signal and a signal aspect.

Signal aspect: *See* **Aspect**

Slip switch: An arrangement of tracks that combines a crossing and a switch using multiple sets of points and frogs.

Slow speed: Typically 15 mph.

Spring switch: A switch that is operated by hand but that can accept trailing train movements in either position without risk of derailment. Springs automatically return the position of points to their normal position.

Spur: A side track that is not used for running. It may be used to store cars, locomotives, or other equipment.

Staff: A distinctive rod used to authorize train movements through a specific block. See Chapter 3.

Staff system: A system of authorizing train movements through a block using a distinctive rod, or token, that must be in possession of the train crew. See Chapter 3

Station: A designated location on a railroad used in control of operations and where business may be conducted. A station may include structures such as station buildings and other facilities but is not necessarily a traditional structure.

Switch: A track arrangement consisting of rails, points, and a frog that controls movement between tracks. Ordinary switches have two positions: normal and reverse. In railroad terminology, a switch may be "lined normal" or "lined reverse." If it has been in the reverse position and is moved back to the normal position, it has been "restored to normal."

Timetable: Printed schedules and special instructions regarding the movement of trains. Using the "timetable and train order" system of train control, an "employee timetable" (rather than the common variety issued for the convenience of passengers and shippers) authorized the movement of trains.

Train: An engine with, or without cars or multiple-unit passenger equipment. Traditionally, an engine and cars would have to display marker lamps or flags before being considered a train.

Train order: A paper order issued by an authorized member of railway operating staff, often a train dispatcher, that gives clear and specific instructions regarding the operations of trains. Typically issued on a standard form and may be used to modify, alter, or append operating instructions printed in an employee timetable.

Upper-quadrant semaphore: A semaphore that displays aspects in the upper quadrant.

Yard: A network of tracks used for assembling trains and/or storing cars and other railroad equipment. Movement on yard tracks is generally unsignaled and limited to restricted speed.

Yard limits: A section of line or tracks designated by yard limit signs where operations fall under distinctive rules designed to facilitate switching and related activities as well as mainline movements.

BIBLIOGRAPHY

BOOKS

Aitken, John. *Modern Train Signalling on British Railways.* Glasgow, U.K., n.d.

Audel, Theo. *Audel's New Electric Library.* Vol. VIII. New York, 1930.

Bailey, Colin. *European Railway Signalling.* London, 1995.

Beaver, Roy C. *The Bessemer and Lake Erie Railroad, 1869–1969.* San Marino, CA, 1969.

Blythe, Richard. *Danger Ahead.* London, 1951.

Brignano, Mary, and Hax McCullough. *The Search for Safety.* American Standard, 1981.

Burgess, George H., and Miles C. Kennedy. *Centennial History of the Pennsylvania Railroad.* Philadelphia, 1949.

Cardini, A. *Multiple Aspect Signalling (British Practice).* Reading, U.K., 1963.

Casey, Robert J., and W. A. S. Douglas. *The Lackawanna Story.* New York, 1951.

Challis, W. H. *Principles of the Layout of Signals (British Practice).* Reading, U.K., 1960.

Currie, J. R. L. *The Runaway Train, Armagh 1889.* Newton Abbot, U.K., 1973.

Doyle, Oliver, and Stephen Hirsch. *Railways in Ireland, 1834–1984.* Dublin, 1983.

Droege, John A. *Passenger Terminals and Trains.* New York, 1916.

Farrington, S. Kip., Jr. *Railroading from the Head End.* New York, 1943.

———. *Railroading from the Rear End.* New York, 1946.

———. *Railroading the Modern Way.* New York, 1951.

———. *Railroads at War.* New York, 1944.

———. *Railroads of the Hour.* New York, 1958.

———. *Railroads of Today.* New York, 1949.

General Railway Signal Company. *Elements of Railway Signaling: A Half-Century of Signaling Progress, 1904–1954.* Rochester, NY: General Railway Signal Company, 1979.

———. *History of General Railway Signal Company.* Rochester, NY: General Railway Signal Company, 1979.

Hall, Stanley. *Danger Signals.* Surrey, U.K., 1987.

Kichenside, G. M., and Alan Williams. *British Railway Signalling.* 3rd ed. Surrey, U.K., 1975.

Nock, O. S. *Fifty Years of Railway Signalling.* London, 1962.

Pigg, James. *Railway Block Signalling.* London, [1900?]

Phillips, Edmund J., Jr. *Railroad Operation and Railway Signaling.* New York, 1942.

Protheroe, Ernest. *The Railways of the World.* London, [1920?]

Raymond, William G. *The Elements of Railroad Engineering,* 5th ed. Revised by Henry E. Riggs and Walter C. Sadler. New York, 1937.

Reed, Robert C. *Train Wrecks.* New York, 1968.

Rolt, L. T. C. *Red for Danger.* London, 1955.

Semmens, Peter. *Railway Disasters of the World*. Sparkford, Nr. Yeovil, U.K., 1994.

Signor, John R. *Donner Pass: Southern Pacific's Sierra Crossing*. San Marino, CA, 1985.

Solomon, Brian. *Trains of the Old West*. New York, 1998.

———. *Railroad Stations*. New York, 1998.

———, and Mike Schafer. *New York Central Railroad*. Osceola, WI, 1999.

Such, W. H. *Principles of Interlocking (British Practice)*. Reading, U.K., 1963.

———. *Mechanical and Electrical Interlocking (British Practice)*. Reading, U.K., 1963.

Talbot, F. A. *Railway Wonders of the World*. Vols. 1 & 2. London, 1914.

Tyer's Block Telegraph and Electric Locking Signals, 5th ed. London, 1874.

Vanns, Michael A. *Signalling in the Age of Steam*. Surrey, U.K., 1995.

Winchester, Clarence. *Railway Wonders of the World*. Vols. 1 & 2. London, 1935.

PERIODICALS

Baldwin Locomotives. Philadelphia, PA. [No longer published.]

B&M Bulletin. Woburn, MA.

Home Signal. Champaign, IL.

Jane's World Railways. London.

Journal of the Irish Railway Record Society. Dublin.

Locomotive & Railway Preservation. Waukesha, WI. [No longer published.]

Modern Railways. Surrey, U.K.

Rail. Peterborough, U.K.

RailNews. Waukesha, WI. [No longer published.]

Railroad History, formerly *Railway and Locomotive Historical Society Bulletin*. Boston, MA.

Railway Age. Chicago and New York.

Railway Gazette. (1870–1908). New York.

Railway Signaling and Communications. Formerly *The Railway Signal Engineer*; originally *Railway Signaling*. Chicago and New York.

Official Guide to the Railways. New York.

Today's Railways. Sheffield, U.K.

Trains. Waukesha, WI.

Vintage Rails. Waukesha, WI. [No longer published.]

OTHER SOURCES

Association of American Railroads. *American Railway Signaling Principles and Practices*. New York, 1937.

Bessemer and Lake Erie Railroad Company. *Special Instructions and Operating Rules*. 1995.

Boston and Maine Railroad. *Time Table No. 41*. 1946.

Burlington Northern Santa Fe Railway. *Train Dispatcher's, Operator's and Control Operator's Manual*. 2001.

D. C. Buell. *The Railway Educational Bureau Instruction Papers, Units CS. 3 to CS. 13: Railway Signaling*. Omaha, NE, 1949.

Chicago Operating Rules Association. *Operating Guide*. [1994?]

CSX Transportation. *Baltimore Division, Timetable No. 2*. 1987.

———. *Signal Apect and Indication Rules*. 2001.

General Code of Operating Rules, 4th ed. 2000.

General Railway Signal Company. *Centralized Traffic Control, Type H, Class M, Coded System, Handbook 20*. Rochester, NY, 1941.

Long Island Rail Road. *Rules of the Operating Department*. 2001.

Metro-North Railroad. *Rules of the Operating Department*. 1999.

———. *Timetable No. 1*. 2001.

New York Central System. *Rules for the Government of the Operating Department*. 1937.

New York and Long Branch Railroad. *Automatic Block and Interlocking Signals*. 1906, reprinted 1975.

NORAC Operating Rules 7th ed. 2000.

The Railway Signal Co. Ltd. *Control of Traffic on Railways*. London, n.d.

Richmond, Fredericksburg and Potomac Railroad Company. *Timetable No. 31*. 1962.

Santa Fe. *Signal Training*. Vols. 1 & 2. 1977.

Thomas Cook, European Timetable, Peterborough, U.K.

Union Pacific. *System Timetable, No. 6*. 1982.

INDEX

Alstom, 62–63
American Association of Railroads, 20, 48
American Railway Association, 47, 147
Amtrak, 7, 59, 64, 105, 113, 133, 138, 142
    Acela Express, 142
    Lake Shore Limited, 7, 105
Aspects, 14, 20–21
    Standard, 47–49
Automatic block signals (ABS), 32–42, 63, 69, 94–117,
    123, 126, 133
        Absolute permissive block (APB), 52, 62–66, 102,
            114–117, 125, 133, 152
        Automatic enclosed disc ("banjo signal"), 35–37
        Bridges, 110
        Closed-circuit system, 34
        Four-aspect, 107–108
        Grade signals, 103
        Location, 109–110
        Masts, 110, 113
        Multiple-aspect, 103–106
        Placement, 113
        Stop and proceed, 102–103
Automatic train control, 137–140
Automatic train stop, 137–140
Ball signals, 18
Baldwin, William A., 34
Baltimore & Ohio (B&O), 7, 28, 34–35, 60, 62, 65, 67, 79,
    82, 84, 86, 88, 102
        Chicago & Alton, 62
        Staten Island Rapid Transit, 62
Banner signals, 37–38
Belt Railway of Chicago (BRC), 131
Bessemer & Lake Erie, 73, 75, 77, 121
Block signals, 23, 31–33, 100
Block system, 31–33, 69
BLS Railway, 51
Boston Elevated Railway, 137
Boston, Revere Beach & Lynn, 137
Boston & Albany (B&A), 38–39, 42–43, 89, 106, 123, 130
    Albany Flyer, 38
Boston & Lowell, 39
Boston & Maine (B&M), 18, 19, 29, 31, 37, 66, 126–127
Brighton Railway, 26
British Rail HST, 105
Brunel, Isambard, 26
Bull, William, 33
Burlington (Chicago, Burlington & Quincy) (Burlington
    Northern Santa Fe), 64, 122, 138
    Advance Flyer, 138
Cab signals, 43, 96, 106, 140–142
    Advanced Civil Speed Enforcement System (ACSES),
        142
    Style-DM (US&S) code transmitter relay, 139
Canadian National, 39, 52, 155
Canadian Pacific, 39
Central Vermont Railway, 18, 19, 29
Chatham and Dover Railway, 33
Chesapeake & Ohio, 52, 63, 110, 142
Chicago & North Western (C&NW), 20, 24, 39, 47, 83,
    97, 106–109, 115, 122, 138, 140–141
Churchill, Dr. William, 48, 57
Civil War (American), 30, 40
Color-light signals, 14, 31, 37, 45–56, 50–52, 55–57, 67,
    103, 106–108, 110–113, 127, 129, 142
        Type D, 106
        Style-TR (US&S), 52
Color-position-lights, 49, 60–65, 67, 86, 103
Colorado Railroad Museum, 23
Conrail, 43, 49, 66, 123, 130
Cooke, William Fothergill, 26, 28
    Telegraphic Railways, 26
Corning Glass, 48, 50, 57
Cotton Belt Railroad, 128
CSX, 60, 62–63, 65–66, 79, 82, 84, 115, 127
CTC (Centralized Traffic Control), 7, 25, 45, 49, 52,
    62–67, 77, 84, 91, 96, 118–123, 125–133, 135
        Arrangement, 120–122
        Double-track, 126–127
        Radio dispatching, 132–133
        Single-track, 122–123, 125
        "Traffic Master" boards, 131
DBAG, 62
Delaware & Hudson Railroad, 29, 30, 151
Denver & Rio Grande Western (DR&GW) (Rio Grande),
    9, 45, 52, 120
Detroit, Toledo & Ironton, 93
Direct Traffic Control, 114, 133, 135
East Lancashire Railway, 68
Eastern Railroad, 39

Electric staff system, 31
Erie Railroad, 7, 20, 29, 49, 113
Farmer, John, 23
Federal Railroad Administration, 138
Frogs, 122
General Code of Operating Rules, 99, 133
General Railway Signal (GRS), 9, 10, 25, 42, 45, 47,
    48–49, 52, 55, 62–64, 83, 84, 109, 115–116, 122, 131,
    138, 148, 152
        Model 2A (semaphore), 48–49, 109, 115
Grade-crossing signals, 6, 36, 96, 144–155
        Automatic gates, 146, 149, 155
        Crossbucks, 146, 151–152, 155
        Frequency-shift overlay (audio frequency overlay), 152
        Gantry, 149
        Masts, 151
        Tunable joint coupler, 153
        Wigwags, 147, 149, 155
Grand Central Terminal, 6, 50
Great Northern Railway (U.K.), 22–23
Great Western Railway (GWR), 17, 26, 33, 47
Gregory, Charles Hutton, 19, 23
Griswold Signal Company, 148, 150
Guilford Rail System, 127
Hall, Thomas Seavey, 36, 38–40
Hall (Switch &) Signal Company, 36, 42, 52, 55, 62, 96,
    113
        Hall disc signal, 20, 36–40, 106
Home Signal newsletter, 7
Hoop, 30–31
Houghton, Alanson B., 48
Iarnród Éireann (Irish Rail), 71, 74, 80
ICE (Germany), 142
Illinois Central, 42, 48, 52, 62, 88, 138
    Cannonball, 42
Institution of (Railway) Signal Engineers, 43, 56
Interlocking plants, 76, 79–88
Interlocking signals, 23, 36, 79–93, 111–112
        All-relay, 84–85
        Electric, 82
        Electro-mechanical, 82
        Electronic, 84
        Electropneumatic, 83
        Mechanical, 81
        Route locking, 86–87
        Towers, 91–93
Interlocking (signal) tower ("signal box"), 24, 79
Interstate Commerce Commission (ICC), 49, 119, 137–138
Jones, Casey, 42
Lackawanna, 52
Liverpool & Manchester, 10
London & South Western railway, 55
London and Croydon Railway, 19, 23
London, Brighton & South Coast Railway
Long Island Rail Road, 50, 59
Loree, L. F., 60
Magnetic Signal Company, 147
Manual block, 28, 32–33, 41, 64, 68–77, 96
        Advanced systems, 72–75
            Single-track, 75–76
        Communication Codes, 76–77
        Controlled, 76
        Permissive, 72
Massachusetts Bay Transportation Authority, 89
Metra (Chicago), 83, 85
Metro-North, 136, 141, 143
Michigan Central Railroad, 39
Milwaukee Road, 20, 52, 55, 83, 85, 117, 122–123, 138
    Hiawatha, 138
Minot, Charles, 29–30
Montana Rail Link, 10
Morse, Samuel Finley Breese, 28
New Haven Railroad, 7, 20, 39–40, 42, 48, 90, 113,
    141–142
New York Central, 6, 7, 35, 48, 50, 52, 55, 62–64, 86, 91,
    105, 110, 126–127, 138, 141
        Water Level Route, 52, 55, 62–63, 126
New York Railroad Club, 48
New York, Susquehanna & Western, 17
Newcastle and Frenchtown Railroad, 17
Nickel Plate Road, 52, 70, 91
Norfolk & Western (N&W), 56, 59
Norfolk Southern, 15, 59, 73, 127, 129
North American Safety Cab, 155
North London Railway, 24
Northeast Operating Rules Advisory Committee
    (NORAC), 88, 98, 104, 106, 108, 111–112, 114
Northern Pacific, 132
Patenall, Frank, 60

Penn-Central, 6
Pennsylvania Railroad (PRR), 25, 34, 39–40, 42, 49, 56–57,
    59, 62, 66, 83, 105, 109, 132, 137–139
        Pennsylvania Station, 137
        Philadelphia and Erie Railroad, 33–34
        Standard signal aspects–circa 1941, 58
        United New Jersey Canal and Railroad Companies, 25,
            31
Pneumatic Signal Company, 62–63
Position-light signals, 6, 56–59, 105
Positive Train Control (Precision Train Control (PTC),
    143
Preece, William, 31
Railway Clearing House, 47
Railway Signal Association, 48
Railway Signal Company, 75, 80
Reading Railroad, 39
Regulation of Railways Act, 32
Robinson, William, 33–35
Rock Island Line, 22, 120, 132
"Rocker and gridiron," 24
Rudd, Arthur Holley, 56–57, 59–60
Rutland Railway, 30
Route signaling, 13
Santa Fe Railway (Burlington Northern Santa Fe), 15, 52,
    55, 103, 110, 122, 125, 131, 138, 140, 146–147
Saxby, John, 23–24
Saxby & Farmer, 84
Scripture, E. W., 48
Searchlights, 6, 13, 31, 52–55, 67, 106, 122, 125
        "Spredlite" lens, 54
Semaphores, 6, 7, 11, 13, 15, 19–23, 31–34, 38–43, 46,
    48–50, 52, 55, 57, 59–60, 66–67, 96–97, 99, 102, 109,
    113, 115, 140, 147
        Electropneumatic, 39
        Intermediate automatic block, 20
        Lower-quadrant, 14, 19, 21–23, 30–33, 38–39, 42–43,
            48–49, 52, 96, 99, 102, 113
        Masts, 21
        Model 2A (General Railway Signal), 48–49, 109, 115
        "Smash boards", 40
        Style-B ("style B") (US&S), 7, 11, 13, 31, 96, 99, 147
        Style-K (Hall Switch & Signal Company), 96
        Style-S ("style S") (US&S), 7, 20, 49
        Style-T ("style T") (US&S), 15
        Style T-2 (US&S), 140
        Upper-quadrant, 14, 19–20, 32, 42–43, 48–49, 55, 96,
            115, 140
Shinkansen, 142
Siemens & Haske, 35
Soo Line, 52, 55, 125
South Shore Railroad, 52
Southern Pacific (SP), 7, 13, 33, 36, 62, 95, 108, 110, 120,
    125–126, 130, 135
Speed signaling, 13, 49, 87–89
Stevens, J. J., J. J. F., and W. A., 24
Stockton & Darlington, 10
Taylor Signal Company, 62–63
Telegraph, 26–31, 63, 69
TGV (France), 142
Tiltboard signals, 17
Track circuits, 96–101
        Relays, 100–101
Train order signal, 23
Tyer, Edward, 31
Union Electric Signal Company, 34
Union Pacific (UP), 35, 40, 52, 62, 93, 95, 119, 126, 130,
    138, 148
Union Railroad, 121
Union Switch & Signal Company, The (US&S), 17,
    34–39, 42, 49, 52, 55, 59–60, 62–64, 83, 96, 99, 102, 110,
    121, 125, 127–128, 138–140, 142, 147
United States Railroad Administration (USRA), 137
        Automatic Train Control Committee, 137
Vail, Alfred, 28
VR (Finnish state railway), 128
Wabash Railroad, 129
Welch, Ashbel, 25, 31, 32
Western Pacific (WP), 125
Westinghouse, George, 34
Westinghouse (Automatic) Airbrake, 13, 39–40
Wheatstone, Charles, 26, 28
Wight, Sedgwick N., 63
Wisconsin Central, 52, 124
Wisconsin & Southern, 154
World War I, 43, 49, 137
World War II, 64, 66, 123, 127, 138

CPSIA information can be obtained
at www.ICGtesting.com
Printed in the USA
LVOW06s0959150416

483472LV00013B/13/P